ABOUT THE AUTHOR

Dr Danny Penman is a meditation teacher and award-winning writer and journalist. He is co-author of the international bestseller *Mindfulness: A Practical Guide to Finding Peace in a Frantic World*. In 2014, he jointly won the British Medical Association's Best Book (Popular Medicine) Award for *Mindfulness for Health: A Practical Guide to Relieving Pain, Reducing Stress and Restoring Wellbeing*. His books have been translated into more than 30 languages. He has received journalism awards from the RSPCA and the Humane Society of the United States. His work has appeared in the *Daily Mail*, the *Guardian*, the *Telegraph* and *New Scientist*. He has also researched and produced documentaries for the BBC and Channel 4.

T0349255

MINDFULNESS
FOR A MORE
CREATIVE
LIFE

Calm your busy mind,
enhance your creativity and
find a happier way of living

DANNY PENMAN

PIATKUS

PIATKUS

First published in Great Britain in 2015 as
Mindfulness for Creativity by Piatkus
This revised edition published in 2021 by Piatkus

5 7 9 10 8 6 4

A CIP catalogue record for this book
is available from the British Library.

ISBN 978-0-349-40823-1

Typeset in Sabon by M Rules
Printed and bound in Great Britain by Clays Ltd, Elcograf S.p.A.

Papers used by Piatkus are from well-managed forests
and other responsible sources.

Piatkus
An imprint of
Little, Brown Book Group
Carmelite House
50 Victoria Embankment
London EC4Y 0DZ

An Hachette UK Company
www.hachette.co.uk

www.littlebrown.co.uk

Dedicated to Luka Phoenix Penman

CONTENTS

ACKNOWLEDGEMENTS

This book could not have been written without a network of people who generously gave their time, help and support throughout.

I am enormously grateful to Sheila Crowley at Curtis Brown and to Anne Lawrance and her team at Piatkus. Thanks also to Anne Newman for copy editing this book and to Jillian Stewart for guiding it through the editorial process. A special 'thank-you' must go to Mark Williams, Emeritus Professor of Clinical Psychology at the University of Oxford. Mark was my co-author on the bestselling *Mindfulness* and taught me much of what I know about meditation and its psychological underpinnings. He gave me the encouragement needed to write this book. I'd also like to thank Ratnaguna at Breathworks in Manchester, for training me how to teach others to meditate. Vidyamala Burch at Breathworks gave lots of help and guidance too. Mark Leonard of the Mindfulness Exchange was a great sounding board for ideas. A great many other people also gave me their time to discuss ideas. Chief amongst these were Gunnery Sergeant Chris Dixon (Rtd.) and Jared Smyser of the US Marine Corps. Colleen Mizuki of the Mind Fitness Training Institute gave me lots of help in this area too. Thanks also to Professor Ellen Langer of Harvard University, Dr Jonathan Greenberg of the Harvard Medical School, Dr Viviana Capurso of the University of Rome, Dr Brian D. Ostafin of the University of Groningen, Dr Fadel Zeidan of the Wake Forest School of Medicine, and Dr Lorenza S. Colzato of Leiden University. All gave their valuable time to discuss ideas with me. Sandra Finkel of Intentional Balance, Michigan, generously gave her time to discuss the implications of the Resilience meditation (see www.sandrafinkel.com).

And, lastly, I must thank my wife Bella, for putting up with me whilst I was engrossed in thought, and our daughter, Sasha, who always ensured that I swiftly returned to the real world.

FOREWORD BY MARK WILLIAMS

The explosion of interest in mindfulness over the last few years has been extraordinary. Many millions of people around the world are now being introduced to some of the ancient wisdom traditions of Asia. No one has *told* these people to become interested or engaged in these traditions, so why the excitement?

People have been inspired not just by the *idea* of stillness in a frantic world, but by the discovery that there are *practices* through which such stillness can be cultivated day by day. The word mindfulness means 'lucid awareness' – a sense of knowing what you are doing as it is happening, moment by moment. Many people find that cultivating mindfulness through regular meditation practice transforms their lives by bringing a sense of peace, of having more time, of feeling less hectic.

The mainstream usage of mindfulness practice in the West started with Jon Kabat-Zinn's work in the University of Massachusetts Medical Center in 1979. He founded a clinic (now called the Center for Mindfulness in Medicine, Healthcare and Society) so that physicians could refer patients who were suffering from long-term medical conditions to an eight-week programme of weekly classes in mindfulness-based stress reduction (MBSR). According to the physicians, finding remedies for these patients had previously proved extremely difficult: the usual medicines had been ineffective, and further surgery was often not an option. But why refer such patients – who were suffering from serious *physical* problems – to a course of mindful awareness? How on earth might this help them? Surely they were already acutely aware of their pain, so how could increased awareness benefit them? And yet the research conducted at the clinic showed that the programme was highly effective in reducing the patients' stress, helping them to find new ways to manage their pain and increasing the overall quality of their lives.

In the early 1990s, Zindel Segal, John Teasdale and myself adapted the eight-week programme for use in mental health settings. We called this new course 'mindfulness-based cognitive therapy' (MBCT). It was specifically designed for people who were vulnerable to depression in the hope that it would reduce their susceptibility to future episodes. Depression is a hidden scar, often suffered in silence by people who are ashamed to admit that they are feeling inexplicably sad, hopeless and down-hearted; that they have no energy and find it impossible to enjoy life any more. It can have a dramatic effect on eating and sleeping, increasing fatigue and destroying concentration and memory. And the sufferer's sense of worthlessness can lead to suicidal thoughts – the idea that everyone would be better off if they were dead. Once again, some may ask how on earth mindful awareness might help? Surely, if anything, those people who are vulnerable to depression are already *too* aware of their moods, and tend to brood about how sad and unworthy they are. Yet research from all around the world has shown that the eight-week MBCT programme reduces the risk of further depression by half in the most seriously vulnerable people. This means that it is at least as effective as any leading antidepressant. As a result, the UK government's National Institute for Health and Care Excellence (NICE) has recommended MBCT for the prevention of recurrent depression since 2004.

What is happening here, and how is it relevant to creativity? This book aims to answer those questions. Only when we resolve the paradox of how the practice of mindfulness works to alleviate physical or mental suffering will we understand how it might help in everyday contexts, too: when our energy levels fall; when we are unable to find the solutions to problems; and when we become entangled in old habits. Those suffering from serious clinical conditions and the rest of us who sometimes feel daunted by everyday challenges share a tendency to get stuck because our minds turn to old habits in a bid to resolve our problems. This happens without us even being aware of it, and only leaves us feeling *more* trapped. Note the previous sentence: we are trapped by processes *of which we are not aware*. Addressing this issue is key to resolving the paradox. Mindfulness training shines a light of awareness not on the pain or the sadness, but on the mind's hidden processes that cause us to get stuck.

In this book, Danny Penman shows how getting stuck in old habits – and then blaming ourselves when we do – impairs creativity. He explains how even small events in our everyday lives can trigger reactions that do not serve us very well. Such reactions are perfectly natural. We want the world to be a certain way, so if an experience is pleasant, we want it to last; and if it doesn't, we feel disappointed. On the other hand, if an experience is unpleasant, we want it to end as soon as possible; and if it doesn't, we begin to wonder how long it will last, and what will happen if it *never* ends.

These habitual reactions can be large and obvious or small and subtle, but they often continue to drive our behaviour long after the circumstance that triggered them has come to an end. Trying to get everything to conform to our view of how it *should* be can be exhausting: we end up overthinking, 'living in our heads' and losing touch with reality. Constantly wanting the world to be a certain way impoverishes our experience of life as it actually is. Our happiness becomes narrowly dependent on certain things turning out *exactly* as we hope they will, and we find it impossible to react with any sort of flexibility when they do not.

Only when we see these habits of the mind clearly, and recognise the many ways in which we might be drawn into their traps, can we disengage from them and free ourselves from their power. As Danny says in this book, 'Understanding your own mind – and how it unwittingly ties itself in knots – is one of the central skills of mindfulness. At its core, mindfulness is about accepting that we are neither perfect nor all-knowing creatures. Our minds can often be noisy and irrational places. But in the quiet spaces in between can lie moments of piercing insight.'

This book is about finding those quiet spaces in between. It reviews the ever-increasing evidence that mindfulness training can release us from the old habits that impair our sense of playfulness and creative insight. Moreover, Danny provides a programme of weekly meditations and habit releasers that anyone can use to experience for themselves what happens when we learn to act in a more flexible way, see our thoughts as mental events, and treat our own minds and bodies with more warmth and compassion. Examples from participants who have practised the meditations will help readers to understand what they need to do to cultivate the stillness out of which creative insights can begin to flow again.

Many of us are able to recall times in our lives when we felt more creative than we do now. Where did that inspiration go? Try as we might, it seems hard – if not impossible – to encourage the creativity to flow again. We start to blame ourselves for our lack of inspiration as our inner critic takes hold. This then becomes a vicious circle, because too much thinking, too much self-criticism, drowns out the quiet voice of creative insight. Instead, we need to change the atmosphere in our minds and hearts. This takes patience, and a willingness to commit oneself to a daily practice, as Danny makes clear in the pages that follow.

Whether you work in the creative industries or in a job that demands outside-the-box thinking, or if you simply want your life to be less hectic and more playful for the sake of your friends, partner or children, this book offers invaluable help.

Mark Williams
Emeritus Professor of Clinical Psychology
University of Oxford

CHAPTER ONE

Hole in the Head

The buzz of creativity always hit Jess around 10 a.m. For some reason, she'd spend the first hour or so of each day batting away pointless emails and staring blankly out of the window. But then her mind would suddenly clear, almost as if a veil had been lifted from her awareness. She'd straighten up in her chair, her pupils would dilate and she'd feel tingly all over. After a sigh, she'd begin typing furiously.

Nothing compared to that magical hour when everything flowed quite naturally. She didn't consciously think or plan. The words seemed to pour through her fingers and on to the computer screen. All of her fears, worries and problems simply melted away, leaving her in complete control of her life and work.

But then something would shatter her concentration: the phone would ring, a text would arrive or a 'vital' email would flash on to her screen. The veil would then draw across her mind and that would be the end of her creativity for the day.

Why can't I just think clearly like that all of the time? she'd snap at herself when her creative bubble had just burst. Resentment would begin gnawing away at her soul. *Clearly I am creative. Nobody achieves as much as me when I'm in the flow. I do more in that hour than the rest of the day put together ... Even if I could work and be as creative as that for just another hour or two each day, then life would be so much better. I'd get a pay rise. I could get a decent car, maybe a house ...*

Jess would then sigh before starting to deal with the pointless dross that cluttered up her workday as a copywriter for a marketing agency.

It's not just copywriters who battle against the mental clutter that destroys their creativity. We all do. And it comes at a huge but largely hidden price. Designers and engineers fail to see cheap and elegant solutions to problems. Doctors miss subtle but important symptoms that cost patients their lives. Managers and entrepreneurs are too frazzled to take advantage of evolving markets. Writers, artists and performers fail to connect with their audiences' souls. Even those who work from home inadvertently strangle their own productivity by forcing themselves into a creative black hole.

This is a book about how you can enhance your own creativity and retake control of your life. It will teach you how to sweep away the barriers that are clouding your mind and throttling your creativity. It will help you make better decisions and deal more effectively with problems. In short, it will help to extend your own magical hour of creativity into two, three or four hours ... or perhaps into whole days. The techniques aren't only used by 'creatives', major businesses, such as Apple, Google and Intel, as well as financiers at J.P. Morgan, HSBC and Deutsche Bank, have adopted them to help them make better decisions. Even the US Marines use them. Truth is, we're all creatives now – whether we want to be or not.

To enhance creativity and problem solving you need to cultivate three skills. Firstly, you need an open but disciplined mind that can gather and then integrate new ideas, concepts and information. This is known as 'divergent thinking' and it happens on both the conscious and unconscious levels. Secondly, you need to consciously notice the new ideas created by your mind and to realise their significance (otherwise they will simply pass you by). And thirdly, you need the courage to follow your ideas wherever they should lead – and the resilience to cope with the inevitable attacks and setbacks.

The practices in the following pages foster all three skills. They are based on ancient traditions dating back at least 2500 years, and were originally developed by the Stoic philosophers of ancient Greece and the early Buddhists. Over the centuries they have been adapted to suit the times, but the core principles have always remained intact. The state of mind they cultivate is known as 'mindfulness', but it has also been called 'awakening', 'presence' or simply 'awareness'. Mindfulness is a state of calm, open-hearted, non-judgmental awareness. It's a state of mind where you are paying full attention to whatever is happening in the present moment, rather than living in the past or worrying about the future. Although it is traditionally developed through mindfulness meditation, other, less formal practices can also be used. This book teaches both.

INSIGHT ...

In recent years, scientists have discovered that practising certain forms of mindfulness meditation for ten to twenty minutes a day can enhance creativity, problem solving and decision making (see box on pages 5–6). They also dissolve anxiety, stress and depression, while enhancing happiness, wellbeing and resilience. A typical ten-minute meditation consists of focusing your attention on the sensations the breath makes as it flows into and out of the body (see page 59). This creates a calm mental space from which you can observe all of your thoughts, feelings and emotions as they bubble up from your deep subconscious. It allows you to watch as they appear in your mind, linger for a while and then dissolve. In effect, your mind becomes less frantic and 'noisy' and this, in turn, means you can notice your quieter thoughts and ideas. So it helps foster great clarity of thought. In this way, mindfulness smooths the path of ideas as they arise from the deepest reaches of your mind. This enhances divergent thinking – the purest form of creativity – and the type that most of us would recognise *as* 'creativity' itself (more about this in Chapter Two). Divergent thinking is the most mysterious state of mind because it appears to conjure up ideas from nowhere – often out of the blue, and frequently without bidding. It's the form of awareness that gave rise to Archimedes' 'Eureka' moment, Isaac Newton's insights into gravity, Einstein's Special Theory of Relativity and many great novels, such as *Dr Jekyll and Mr Hyde*. In short, it's the state of awareness that allows you to spontaneously 'see' the solution to a problem, to conjure up new ideas and to create a work of art or design with true insight and flair.

The benefits of mindfulness meditation

Thousands of peer-reviewed scientific papers prove that mindfulness improves mental and physical wellbeing while also enhancing creativity and decision making. Here are some of the main findings:

- Mindfulness improves creativity.[1]

- Mindfulness improves attention span, working memory and reaction speed. It also enhances mental stamina and resilience.[2]

- Mindfulness enhances decision making.[3]

- Meditation enhances brain function. It increases grey matter in areas associated with self-awareness, empathy, self-control and attention.[4] It soothes the parts of the brain that produce stress hormones[5] and builds those areas that lift mood and promote learning.[6] It even reduces some of the thinning of certain areas of the brain that 'naturally' occurs with age.[7]

- Mindfulness is a potent antidote to anxiety, stress, depression, exhaustion and irritability. In short, regular meditators are happier and more contented, while being far less likely to suffer from psychological distress.[8]

- Mindfulness is at least as good as drugs or counselling for the treatment of clinical-level depression. One structured programme known as Mindfulness-Based Cognitive Therapy (MBCT) is now one of the preferred treatments recommended by the UK's National Institute for Health and Care Excellence. [9]

- Meditation improves the immune system. Regular meditators are admitted to hospital less often for cancer, heart disease and numerous infectious diseases.[10]

- Meditation improves heart and circulatory health by reducing blood pressure and lowering the risk of hypertension. It also reduces the risks of developing and dying from cardiovascular disease and lowers its severity should it arise.[11]

- Mindfulness is very beneficial for chronic pain. Studies show that pain 'unpleasantness' can be reduced by 57 per cent. Experienced meditators can reduce it by 93 per cent.[12]

- The benefits of meditation begin to take root in the brain after just a few minutes of practice.

DIVERGENCE . . .

Mindfulness enhances such divergent thinking on another level too. It progressively dissolves the mental habits that force us to think along the same tired, old lines over and over again. These habits exert immense control over our lives, but we are largely unaware of their influence. In fact, scientists estimate that around 45 per cent of the choices and decisions we make each day are governed by habit.[13] Such habits have their uses, but they are very much a double-edged sword. On the one hand, they allow the mind to outsource routine matters to its 'autopilot', so that we can focus on the more important things. On the other hand, they can lock in place the ways in which we approach the world and think about ideas and problems. In short, they can stifle creativity.

And here's the rub: because habits allow you to outsource certain forms of thinking to your autopilot, often without you realising it, thinking itself can become increasingly habitual. Certain thoughts can become habits in themselves. Negative, self-defeating thought patterns are particularly habitual. Ones such as *Why can't I do this?*, *What's wrong with me today?* or *He's got it in for me* can turn into mental soundbites that the autopilot throws into your mind just as easily as it helps you brush your teeth or find your way to work. The same is true for countless other thought patterns too.

The way that we tackle problems at work and at home is often governed by thought patterns laid down many years before. They originally served a purpose, but do they still? Technology may allow us to tackle problems in new ways, but do our patterns of thought and behaviour? Circumstances may change, but our patterns of thought and behaviour often do not. This is why it is so easy – and so seductive – to think along the same tired, old, familiar lines and to make the same decisions over and over again. In this way, habitual thought patterns can progressively narrow the mind and ensure that we consciously think less and less, while ceding more and more control to our mental autopilot.

This is why around half of the choices and decisions we all make each day are governed by habit. If this figure seems a little high, cast an eye over your own life: do you always sleep on the same side of the bed? Have sex on the same nights of the week (and in the same positions)? Do you wake up at the same time each day? Always take the same number of footsteps to the bus stop, station or car? Take the same route to work? And when you're there, do you always sit in the same chair at meetings, drink out of your 'favourite' cup and have the same polite conversations with the same people?

When it comes to approaching problems, habitual ways of thinking can make it very difficult to create innovative solutions or to spark a chain of new or original ideas. But there is an alternative. Habits aren't destiny (unless you allow them to be). You can progressively disentangle yourself from the web of habits that controls your life by using the meditations in this book. And when you do so, you'll find it increasingly easy to think clearly, spot new ideas and adapt to changing circumstances. In the long run, this will allow you to consciously 'jump the tracks' into more fruitful ways of thinking.

Mindfulness is ...

- paying full conscious attention to whatever thoughts, feelings and emotions are flowing through your mind without harsh judgment or criticism

- being fully aware of whatever is happening in the present moment and not being trapped in the past or worrying about the future

- living *in* the moment, not *for* the moment.

Thinking is not a problem. Thinking while being unaware that you are thinking can become a major problem.

RESILIENCE ...

It is not enough to think clearly and to produce original ideas. You also need the courage to follow them wherever they should lead and the resilience to withstand failure, hardship and cynicism. The scientific evidence is clear: mindfulness helps build such courage and resilience.[14] It does this by encouraging the mind's harsh 'inner critic' to fall silent for a while. Your inner voice is an essential part of your identity, but if it becomes too dominant, then it can stifle free-flowing creativity and experimentation. Left unchecked, your mind can start baiting itself with such bitter and angry thoughts as, *This is pointless. I'm just not up to it any more ... I can't come up with anything new at all. Why can't I just make a decision and get on with it?* Your inner critic can all too easily consume all of your energy, leaving behind a burnt-out shell. You can start to become paralysed with indecision and even the smallest of problems can seem insurmountable. This not only further erodes creativity, but left unchecked it can lead to anxiety, stress, depression and exhaustion.

But it doesn't have to be this way. As you read through this book you will come to understand that your inner voice is not always correct. The mind's running commentary on the world should not be mistaken for the mind itself. In short, thoughts are not always facts (even those that claim to be). Simply understanding how this aspect of your mind works can reinvigorate creativity and grant you the courage to experiment, to make decisions and to risk failure in pursuit of your goals.

Such courage, especially in the face of failure, is essential. After all, you simply cannot create something new or make a difficult decision without risking failure – and taking such risks requires great courage. Creativity, problem solving and effective decision making all require a special type of quiet, persistent courage. It's not the flavour of courage that is bold or arrogant. It's far more subtle than that. It's the type that you feel when you are standing on solid ground; when you have a sense of wholeness, certainty and strength; of trusting that there is a path to your goal, even though it might not be obvious at the time. Mindfulness cultivates such courage by broadening your mental horizons so that everything falls naturally into perspective. It's as if you can see the world for miles around and all of your fears, worries and problems simply dissolve. You come to understand that most problems, no matter how difficult they might at first appear, are often akin to bumps in the road, rather than life-and-death scenarios. This, in turn, fosters the courage necessary to create new ideas and follow them wherever they should lead.

Mindfulness is not a religion

- It is simply a form of mental training.

- It will not deaden your mind, but will instead make you more creative, less stressed and more effective at decision making.

- It does not take a lot of time (around ten to twenty minutes a day is enough).

- It is not difficult or complicated.

- You can meditate virtually anywhere; on buses, trains, aircraft, offices – even in a queue at the supermarket.

FREE THINKING . . .

Mindfulness for a More Creative Life operates on two levels. Firstly, there is the four-week meditation programme, which takes around ten to twenty minutes a day. This clears the mind and allows innovative ideas to take form and crystallise. It also soothes the mind and dissolves stress. This, in turn, allows the mind to work more effectively, so that you can begin to solve problems faster and more intuitively. Mindfulness also helps decision making by dissolving anxiety, stress, frustration and depression. Even if you have none of these problems, you will still find yourself feeling happier, sleeping better and becoming fully engaged with life once again.

Secondly, mindfulness creates a mental vantage point from which you can observe just how much of your life is controlled by habitual ways of thinking and approaching the world. Such renewed clarity will help you tackle the habits that constrain creativity and effective problem solving. Habit breaking (or habit releasing) is as simple as taking a different route to work or spending a little time walking around the park soaking up the sights, sounds and smells. Or it might mean listening to your favourite music with fresh ears or drinking a cup of tea or coffee with your eyes closed. Such simple things broaden awareness, spark curiosity and open the doors to serendipity.

If you want to start the four-week programme right away, you can begin at Chapter Three. If you'd like to understand how the programme works, and the latest scientific discoveries that support it, then carry on reading. I strongly recommend that you do read the following chapter as it underpins the effectiveness of the whole programme. If you're keen to start now, then there's no reason why you can't start the programme immediately while you read the next chapter.

It's best if you read through the meditations first and then listen to the tracks while you actually carry out the meditations. Details of where the meditations can be downloaded can be found on page 41.

CHAPTER TWO

Serendipity

The US Marines sneaked into the Afghan town shortly after dawn. Fanning out through the dusty alleyways, they began to look for a group of insurgents who'd taken refuge in the town the night before. They knew they were there, somewhere, just like the snipers who might begin picking them off, one by one, without warning. When the Marines reached the market stalls in the centre of the town they paused and began looking around warily. Moments later, they were knocked off their feet by an immense shockwave: it was from an exploding IED hidden in a pile of rubbish.

Even through the thick, swirling dust it was clear that all hell had broken loose. Screaming shoppers and stallholders were frantically running away and diving through windows and doorways. The remains of market stalls lay scattered about. The air was thick with the smell of explosive, singed hair, rotting rubbish – and worse.

As the dark smoke began to clear it became apparent that two Marines had been felled by the blast. One lay motionless on the ground, fluid trickling from his ears; the other was screaming incoherently.

'Get the casualties back here,' yelled a Marine from the cover of an empty building. 'Let's go!' But as his comrades desperately tried to evacuate the wounded, a second IED exploded in the market.

The nightmare, it seemed, had only just begun.

This terrifyingly realistic exercise was being staged to prepare a platoon of US Marines for their deployment to Afghanistan. Afterwards, the platoon leader gathered up his troops, two-thirds of whom had never been in combat before, and explained: 'We're giving you these emotions now, so that when it happens for real, you won't be acting so crazy. You'll be able to calm yourselves down.'

A few hours later, the same group of Marines were doing just that: calming down. They were sitting cross-legged on the grass at Camp Pendleton, just outside San Diego, Southern California. It had been a tough day and now it was time for their meditation in the evening sunshine. Each Marine closed his eyes and breathed gently in and out. One by one they started to relax. Their broad shoulders and powerful chests were soon moving in fluid harmony with their breath. Knotted muscles unfurled. Gritted teeth loosened. Their grimy faces were soon the picture of peaceful tranquillity.

Although it makes for an incongruous end to the day, the Marines have begun to embrace mindfulness as part of their training – and they report remarkable results. The Marines are now far better at dealing with anxiety, stress, depression and insomnia. Mindfulness helps them to stay calm and focused in the heat of battle and thereby reduces collatoral damage. It also improves their memory, attention span and 'situational awareness', while also enhancing mental agility, creativity and resilience.[1] As Gunnery Sergeant Chris Dixon told me: 'After the course, I wasn't scatter-brained any more. I was far more in control of my life, no matter how much pressure I was under. I wish I'd learned these techniques years ago as they made me a far more adaptable and effective Marine. I can't think of any aspect of my life that it hasn't helped me with.'[2]

The Marines may be an extreme example, but when we are under pressure our basic survival instincts come to the fore. These instincts may have evolved aeons ago, but they are still at work in all of us, all of the time, whether we are in the thick of battle, struggling to focus on an important project with a tight deadline, or feeling frustrated in a traffic jam. And, strange as it may seem, they are of profound significance when it comes to creativity and problem solving.

Our survival instincts are driven by two powerful emotional-regulation systems known as the 'threat-avoidance' and 'achievement' systems. The threat-avoidance system focuses on the most immediate needs of survival and dictates whether we fight, flee or freeze when we encounter danger (hence its alternative name of the 'fight-or-flight' reflex). It does this by driving such emotions as fear and anger and works by priming reflexes and habits, so that you can react in an instant. It's also deeply primeval in nature, and can, as such, be a bit simplistic in the way that it interprets a threat. In fact, it makes no distinction between a direct physical threat, such as a predator (or an enemy sniper), and a more diffuse mental one, such as the stress created by a difficult boss or an approaching deadline. If you feel under pressure, then this system will take control of your mind whether you want it to or not.

What exactly is creativity?

Creativity is characterised by the ability to perceive the world in new ways, to find hidden patterns, to make connections between seemingly unrelated phenomena and to generate solutions. Creativity involves two processes: thinking, then producing. If you have ideas, but don't act on them, you are imaginative but not creative.[3]

Creative people tend to be more open and enquiring, while being less constrained by existing categories and boundaries. They are generally more autonomous and value curiosity and exploration as ends in themselves. They have flexible minds and ideas are their currency. They value expertise and enjoy pushing their own boundaries and those of others. They love ideas for their own sake and will happily tinker with existing ones or use them as building blocks for entirely new ones. Creative people are not only artists, writers and academics, but are also to be found in science, engineering, business, finance and the law. In fact, creativity is so important – and so innately human – that there is no aspect of life that it can't play a part in.

There are two broad styles of thinking associated with creativity:

Convergent thinking

Convergent thinking is normally logical, rational, deductive and focused. It aims to produce the single best answer to a problem with little or no ambiguity.[4] It emphasises speed, accuracy and logic and concentrates on recognising the familiar, reapplying techniques and accumulating stored information. It is most effective in situations where an answer readily exists and simply needs to be either recalled or worked out using decision-making strategies. The solution that is derived at the end of convergent thinking is generally the best possible answer the majority of the time.

Convergent thinking is linked to knowledge as it involves manipulating existing information or wisdom using standard procedures. Knowledge can be an important aspect of creativity. It is a source of ideas, suggests pathways to solutions and provides criteria for effectiveness and novelty. When you use convergent thinking to solve a problem you will often consciously use standards or probabilities to make judgments. (This contrasts with divergent thinking, where judgment is deferred while looking for and accepting many possible solutions.)

It is an aspect of the mind's Doing mode (see page 35).

Divergent thinking

Divergent thinking is spontaneous and free-flowing. It lies behind the 'purest' forms of creativity and in many ways is *true* creativity. Divergent thinking generates ideas by exploring many possible solutions, often in parallel. Ideas may arise in an emergent cognitive fashion as epiphanies or 'Aha!' moments. Many possible solutions are explored and unexpected connections are drawn. A high IQ alone does not guarantee creativity. Instead, traits that promote this style of thinking are more important, and it is commonly found among people with personality traits such as nonconformity, curiosity, willingness to take risks, courage, persistence and resilience.

Divergent thinking is cultivated by the mind's Being mode (see page 39) and arises most often when the soothing-and-contentment system is ticking over (see page 23).

Creative thought often involves both convergent and divergent thinking. Neither is 'better' or 'worse' than the other, and each has its own qualities. The most creative solutions or ideas, be they in art, science or business, often involve multiple phases and iterations of convergent and divergent thinking. So although the finished idea will often arise in an 'Aha!' moment, divergent thinking shouldn't take all of the credit; convergent thinking might have accumulated the knowledge, wisdom and ideas necessary for divergent thinking do to its unconscious work.

Experiments have shown that mindfulness boosts creativity largely by enhancing divergent thinking, but many of the qualities associated with convergent thinking are also enhanced by mindfulness. Such things as working memory, clarity of thought and mental fortitude, resilience and courage are all boosted by mindfulness and are important features of convergent thinking. Happiness also enhances both convergent and divergent thinking. Mindfulness increases happiness and dissolves anxiety, stress, depression and feelings of exhaustion. It is through this additional route that mindfulness also boosts creativity.

The 'achievement' system, on the other hand, compels you to seek out opportunities and resources. It lies behind such 'get up and go' emotions as desire and competitiveness. It's invigorating – sexy almost – and makes you feel powerful whenever you conjure up a great idea, complete a project on time or beat a competitor in an argument. It packs an enormous emotional punch and explains why success can be so addictive.

These two systems normally interact seamlessly with each other to form your own personal *experience* of the world. In other words, they blend together to create your emotional backdrop and set your mental stage. This ensures that you rarely feel a pure emotion: for example, if you're angry, you might be a little fearful as well and this fear might have a few shades of desire flickering away in the background; or if you're feeling competitive, you might be a little angry and jealous too. Such emotional constellations are entirely normal and naturally wax and wane.

Problems can arise, however, when the two systems drift out of balance with each other. A good example is when you're under a lot of pressure at work. This overstimulates the avoidance system so that you begin to flail around in fight-or-flight mode and become more and more stressed. So you begin to focus your attention on to your immediate fears and worries to the exclusion of all else. This narrows the mind and drives your thoughts around in circles. It also progressively reduces your sense of perspective and puts your emotions on a hair trigger. This begins to limit divergent thinking (which lies at the heart of creativity and effective decision making), so that you can become trapped like a rabbit in a car's headlights (see page 16, 'What exactly is creativity?').

A similar thing happens when the achievement system becomes overactive. You may start driving yourself brutally hard, so that you become increasingly stressed and unhappy. Once again, it compels you to focus your mind on the immediate task. Such intense focus is not inherently problematic – sometimes you need to be focused and driven – but it can become a hindrance when focus turns into tunnel vision and you can no longer see the wood for the trees. If this should happen, then other more effective ways of tackling a problem can slip by unnoticed. Once again, it undermines divergent thinking, so that you can become like a dog worriting at a bone with no end in sight.

NEGATIVITY BIAS

But there is another downside to these two emotional systems: they can force you to focus on the negative – to always look on the bleak side of life. This is because both systems force you to respond to the proverbial 'carrots' and 'sticks' (to seek out rewards and avoid threats) and this process has a powerful inbuilt bias. Evolution has ensured that your attention inevitably focuses first and foremost on threats. This is because if you miss a 'carrot' today – a pleasant experience, say – you'll get another chance tomorrow, whereas if you fail to spot a 'stick', you may die and never get another chance. So nature compels you to always spot the sticks and to avoid them at all costs, even if it means frequently missing the opportunity of a carrot.

This inherent bias towards negative thinking ensures that we tend to see threats everywhere and notice the flaws in everything. And it doesn't matter whether these threats are real or imagined. After all, in evolutionary terms it is far better to always assume the worst – even if we are frequently wrong – than to have a happy-go-lucky attitude which ensures that we are right most of the time, but when we are wrong, we are disastrously wrong. This is the main reason why we tend to focus with laser sharpness on the negative and can easily end up thinking the worst of everyone and everything. Equally importantly, it means that we simply do not notice the overwhelming number of pleasant things in life and the opportunities we're presented with. It's the ultimate opportunity cost.

This 'negativity bias' in the brain is triggered so fast that it sweeps away all before it. Neuroscientists estimate that it takes around a tenth of a second to notice a threat – a suspicious-looking face in a crowd, for example – and many times longer to notice something pleasant. This is compounded by the fact that we react to threats virtually instantaneously and store them in our memories, where they are held on a hair trigger ready for instant recall, while positive experiences take far longer to sink in. In fact, it can take five pleasant experiences to balance a single negative one of equal magnitude. It's as if the brain has Velcro for negative experiences and Teflon for good ones.[5] And this bias is built into the very structure of the brain itself, driving our strongest instincts. It's so powerful that you can actually see this process unfurling in a brain scanner. Negative experiences generate intense activity, while pleasant ones of equal magnitude produce far less. And the amygdala, central to the brain's alarm system, dedicates two-thirds of its neurons to processing negative experiences and far fewer to dealing with positive ones.

In short, evolution has given us a brain that routinely tricks us into overestimating threats and underestimating rewards and opportunities. And while this makes evolutionary sense, it can end up crippling creativity and driving procrastination, not to mention making for a truly miserable existence. But then again, as far as nature is concerned, it is far more important that we survive than we be happy and productive. Nevertheless, this has huge implications for creativity and decision making because it means that you will always lean towards being fearful, towards procrastination, towards playing it safe. After all, you cannot be truly creative if you are frightened, dither endlessly and never take a risk.

Deep down, everyone knows this, but most of us have spent so many years blaming ourselves that we overlook the true culprit: fear cultivated by nature's negativity bias. Writers and artists call it a 'creative block'. However, its true name is *fear*. Others in the creative industries might put it down to laziness. Its real name is *dread*. Business leaders call it procrastination, but that's because they can't admit that they're *frightened*.

The negativity bias ensures that we are all frightened of not being good enough, of failing – but also of succeeding (lest anyone find out it's a failure in disguise). It means that we are all fearful of starting new projects, and also of finishing them. We are also fearful every step of the way. Such fear is genuinely crippling – and it is rammed home by many aspects of daily life. The modern workplace ensures that our performance is constantly measured and our achievements compared to those of others. This creates a lingering sense of fear and risk aversion that undermines the very creativity that is so highly coveted. Even well-meaning work practices that are explicitly designed to reward effort can backfire. By focusing the mind on achievement – to the exclusion of all else – you create a sense of tunnel vision that can all too easily close down the mind and undermine creative thinking. This is because pure creativity is a process, an end in itself – so when it is monitored, controlled or even encouraged with a little too much gusto, it simply evaporates.

If all this sounds a bit, well, negative, it's not meant to be. Rather, it is a message of hope because we *can* train our minds to counteract the negativity bias. We can step outside of our fears and worries. It is possible to cultivate the courage and resilience necessary to succeed and be truly creative. This is because nature has given us another system that allows us to correct the balance and to approach the world in a radically different way. It offers an alternative to becoming locked into either the avoidance or achievement systems on the one hand or of veering wildly between them on the other. It's called the soothing-and-contentment system,[6] and, unexpected as it may seem, it is now being actively cultivated by military training programmes because a fearful fighter is one who makes poor, uncreative and irrational decisions, while one who is courageous makes rational, decisive and creative ones.

When we no longer feel threatened, and when resources are abundant so that we're not struggling to get by, we feel a pleasant, bone-deep contentment. We feel 'quiet', soothed, content and peaceful inside. While these feelings are undoubtedly pleasant, they are also useful. When we feel safe, we become confident enough to look beyond the immediate needs of survival and begin looking outwards through idle curiosity. This allows the mind to gently tick over, to scan the world for interesting new ideas, to weave together hitherto hidden patterns and to conjure up new concepts. It cultivates divergent thinking and the enhanced perspective that this produces lies at the heart of creativity.

This soothing-and-contentment system has many other benefits too. When it's active, it enables us to live in a more connected and harmonious way with those around us. So we can be kinder to ourselves and to others. This bolsters the bonds that encourage us to co-operate rather than compete with each other. Such co-operation was critical for our ancestors because those who worked together were more likely to survive than those who struggled in conflict and isolation.

Yet this inner peacefulness and sense of perspective is totally different from the hyped-up experience that many of us have in the typical workplace. It may appear to be 'soft', almost a sign of weakness, but it is immensely useful in the long run because it is so intimately connected to creativity, emotional intelligence, charisma and the myriad 'soft skills' required for effective management and leadership.[7]

In 2001 Ronald Friedman and Jens Forster at the University of Maryland, USA, decided to investigate these ideas in a now classic experiment.[8] Two groups of students were asked to play a simple game where they had to solve a maze puzzle by drawing a line with a pencil from the middle of the maze to the exit without taking the pencil off the page – you probably did these when you were a child. The goal was to help a cartoon mouse escape, but there was a twist. Friedman and Forster gave one group a version of the maze that had a tasty-looking piece of cheese in front of a mouse hole at the exit. This is known as a positive or approach-orientated puzzle. The other group of students did a version where the cheese had been replaced by an intimidating-looking owl that was poised to swoop and kill the mouse with its talons at any moment. This is known as a negative or avoidance-orientated puzzle, and it primes the mind's threat-avoidance system.

The mazes were simple to do and all of the students easily completed them in a couple of minutes or less. But the effects of doing so on the students' outlooks on life were radically different. When the students took creativity tests, those who'd avoided the owl did 50 per cent *worse* than those who'd helped the mouse find the cheese. This was because the cartoon owl had triggered the students' avoidance systems, which had, in turn, closed down their minds and left them with a lingering fear of failure and an enhanced sense of caution and vigilance. This state of mind had reduced their flexibility, narrowed down their options and hamstrung their creativity. This outlook couldn't have been more different from that of those students who'd helped the mouse find the cheese. They were happy to experiment, were more carefree and open to new experiences and far less cautious. The experience had opened their minds.

Think about the significance of this experiment. If you do something in a fearful, negative or overly driven way, then you will activate the mind's avoidance system. This will narrow the mind and reduce your flexibility. You will become ever more stressed and less adaptable and creative. If, however, you do exactly the same thing in a welcoming and warm-hearted manner, with genuine interest and curiosity, then anxiety, stress and unhappiness will ebb away and be replaced with warmth, creativity and flexibility. So your life will not only become richer and more fulfilling, but more productive too.

It's important to realise that there is nothing 'wrong' with either the threat-avoidance or the achievement system. Nor is there anything inherently problematic with the negativity bias – or anything 'right', 'pure' or 'wholesome' about the soothing-and-contentment system. All are designed to work in harmony with each other, so that you can thrive in an ever-changing and increasingly frantic world. Problems only arise when these systems drift out of harmony with each other. And, unfortunately, it's all too easy for these systems to drift out of sync because of another deeply buried psychological force: the autopilot.

Mindfulness and effective decision making

Mindfulness enhances decision making on multiple levels. According to Dr Natalia Karelaia, Assistant Professor of Decision Sciences at the INSEAD Business School in Paris, mindfulness is being incorporated into 'every area of business where strong decisions are required'. She goes on:

While it's generally accepted that mindfulness helps decision makers to reach conclusions, there's growing evidence that the positive influence goes much further, impacting the way decisions are identified, made, implemented and assessed. Close analysis of the latest mindfulness research suggests that mindfulness techniques can have a positive effect on all of the widely recognised stages of the decision-making process.[9]

There are four main stages to making an effective decision and mindfulness has been shown to help with all of them:

1. **Framing the decision:** sometimes, the best course of action is not to make a decision at all, but instead simply to observe while events take their course. Mindfulness gives you the insight, courage and patience to follow this course of action, where appropriate. If a decision *is* required, then mindfulness can help you clarify your objectives, generate options and avoid irrationally aggravating a previously flawed decision. Mindfulness is extremely effective for avoiding the so-called 'sunk-cost bias'.[10] This is the irrational tendency to continue with a course of action simply because you have already made an investment of time, money or effort. A classic example is the refusal to sell a failing company's shares simply because you hope the share price will recover. In other words, it's when you throw good money after bad. Mindfulness can also help you make more strategic decisions too – those that are more in keeping with your long-term goals and underlying ethics.

2. **Gathering ideas and information:** mindfulness can help you avoid information overload by enhancing working memory and cognition.[11] It can also help you to focus your efforts on gathering the most relevant information available; that which is more likely to be in accordance with a correctly framed decision and your long-term aims. It helps you to avoid habitual search patterns too. This will increase the likelihood of discovering new or unexpected ideas. In addition, mindfulness can help put information in context by enhancing your overall perspective. According to Dr Karelaia, 'Mindful decision makers are also more likely to recognise the limits of their knowledge and to objectively assess uncertainty. In fact, research has found that people who are more mindful have a greater tolerance of uncertainty and are more decisive when faced with making a choice despite many unknowns.'

3. **Coming to a conclusion:** mindfulness reduces 'cognitive rigidity' – the tendency to make decisions using habitual thought patterns.[12] Such cognitive rigidity can seriously impair decision making and force you to 'think *inside* the box'. Mindfulness also helps you to make more rational – and less emotionally biased – decisions. It does this by helping you to sense your emotional landscape and to gauge when it is beginning to bias your decisions.[13] Mindful people also tend to be more intuitive. Intuition arises from unconscious thought processes and can be very effective at dealing with complexity and ambiguity. It often lies behind creative 'Aha!' moments.[14] But equally importantly, mindfulness enhances the courage and resilience necessary to implement decisions.

4. **Learning from experience:** the final stage of decision making is arguably the most important – learning from experience. Accepting mistakes can be particularly difficult. Mindfulness can make this process a little easier because it reduces defensiveness and promotes courage and resilience.

In addition, says Dr Karelaia:

Heightened awareness ensures that mindful individuals may be more likely to learn the right lessons from experience. It's a well-known phenomenon in psychology that we often attribute our past success to our own skill and our past failures to some external circumstance. This can lead to overconfidence, which can be quite disastrous in organisational or entrepreneurial situations. More mindful individuals are more likely to disengage from their ego, making them more open to negative feedback. So mindfulness helps decision makers learn in an unbiased way.

CREATURES OF HABIT

It's not a very comforting thought, but much of what we do each day arises from habits that were hardwired into our brains many years before. To a large extent, they control our taste in food, our sense of fashion and even our choice of partners.[15] They also govern how we approach problems and conjure up new ideas.

Habits are an elegant solution to a fundamental shortcoming in the human brain, namely, a bottleneck in its 'working memory'.

This form of memory has a finite capacity to store and manipulate information. Most people can hold only around seven or eight pieces of information in their conscious mind at any one time (or fewer when under pressure). This is enough to deal with the normal tasks of daily life, but if the working memory becomes overloaded, then the mind slows down as it's forced to juggle more and more thoughts into and out of its longer-term memory. One thought drives out the next, and the next, until the mind becomes increasingly stressed and confused. To help get around this, the brain automates routine tasks by creating habits.

Habits are simply a chain of co-ordinated actions that are needed to carry out a task such as tying your shoelaces or getting dressed in the morning. In this way, a complex routine is compressed down into a single simple one – often no more than a thought – that requires a fraction of the brainpower to carry out. Without them you'd be doomed to consciously plan and perform every single thing that you do each day – from that first cup of coffee in the morning, to finding your way to work, through to cooking your evening meal and brushing your teeth before bed. The brain is very efficient at building habits. If you repeat something more than a couple of times, then the routine begins to wear tracks in the mind: a habit is born. Each time you repeat the habit the track becomes a little deeper. Eventually, the brain lays down a specialised circuit dedicated to performing that habit, meaning that it becomes hardwired into the brain itself. And each time you repeat the habit, this circuit becomes a little stronger, so that it gets progressively easier to trigger the habit and to carry out the routine. Before long, extremely complex routines become effortless. What's more, such habits can be triggered unconsciously. This is why you can suddenly 'wake up' and notice that you are halfway through doing something without realising why (driving to work instead of to a friend's house, for example).

The basal ganglia – a part of the brain that evolved over 500 million years ago – is the seat of the brain's autopilot and it acts like an orchestra conductor, deploying habits in a precise sequence to produce complex behaviour that goes on for a long while.[16] It watches out for triggers, fires up the brain circuits necessary to carry out the habit, then basks in the warm glow of satisfaction reflected from the brain's pleasure centres. This can make habits very seductive and explains why it's so easy to lose control of the autopilot. Another reason is that when a habit emerges, the conscious brain stops participating in decision making. It diverts its attention to other matters – to daydreaming perhaps – so that unless you consciously interrupt a habit, the routine will unfold automatically. The end of the routine might well then act as the trigger for another habit.

In this way, long chains of habits can unfurl one after another without any conscious input at all. In fact, the basal ganglia is capable of co-ordinating routines so complex that we no longer see them as habits at all – they are seen as finely honed skills (or perhaps as aspects of character). Driving is a good example. It's a sequence of countless habits all stitched together into a seamless tapestry. Think back to your first driving lesson. Can you remember the confusion and fear? You had those uncomfortable feelings for good reason: driving is complex and requires a lot of concentration. And yet it becomes so automatic that you've probably forgotten just how difficult it is. The only reason you can drive at all is because your mind is extremely good at automating such complex tasks. And it does so largely through the basal ganglia which, because it is so old in evolutionary terms, can be a little simplistic in the way that it senses triggers and deploys habits. It's also a bit of a hog, with a tendency to take ever more control over your life, albeit with the best of intentions: it wants to streamline life, so that your conscious mind can focus its limited resources on more useful or interesting tasks. Paradoxically, this tendency towards 'mission creep' ensures that habits can become a double-edged sword. On the one hand, they simplify life by automating boring and repetitive routines, but on the other, they can begin controlling so much of daily life that you can become less and less aware of your life as it actually happens (and have correspondingly less conscious control over it).

HABITUAL THOUGHTS

Habits don't just govern behaviour – they can also begin controlling what you think. Repetitive thoughts and routine ways of solving problems wear tracks in the mind in the same way as other routines. Ever struggled to get the chorus of an annoying song out of your mind? Or the recent memory of an embarrassing faux pas? Both are habitual thoughts. And although such thoughts are soon forgotten, other, more emotionally charged ones can begin wearing deeper grooves in the mind. Eventually, these, too, can become hardwired into the structure of the brain. Creative blocks are a good example (although the same underlying principles apply to other situations where you become 'stuck' or unable to solve a problem or tricky situation). In such blocks, the mind becomes trapped by circular thoughts like: *Oh, for God's sake, why can't I just do this? I should be able to ... I just keep on going around in circles. I've really got to work harder and crack this before anyone notices.* One thought triggers the next, and the next, in a repetitive pattern that saps energy and undermines confidence. Such thoughts can lock your mind into a downward spiral that clouds creative insight.

Of course, most people, most of the time, quickly snap out of such blocks. But you can become trapped in one – or lose the ability to make rational decisions, when repetitive thoughts begin to trigger emotionally charged memories. This happens because the mind is designed to spot patterns and 'meaning' in an avalanche of data. So when a thought crosses your mind, the brain digs up memories that reflect such thoughts. It's looking for the reason *why* you feel trapped. It's searching for some patterns – clues that will help it solve the current problem that has ensnared you. In practice, this means that if you are at a creative low ebb, or in fear of failure, then you will start to remember times in the past when you were frightened or failed. Your mind does this in the hope of digging up a solution that worked in the past that can be applied in the present. But it doesn't stop there. It begins to extrapolate such memories into the future. Once again, it does this to try to find a solution, but if you extrapolate a memory tinged with fear into the future, then it becomes a worry. So you end up not only suffering from the current angst of your creative block, but will also remember the bitterness of past failures and 'pre-feel' worries about the future. But it can become even worse than this because such a distressing state of mind can start to overstimulate the threat-avoidance system (see page 15), and when this happens, a vicious cycle can be triggered. Each painful memory triggers the threat-avoidance system a little bit more, which, in turn, triggers more habitual fears, creating more worries about the future. These then dredge up more painful memories.

Brain scans confirm all this. People who rush around mind-lessly – who are trapped inside distressing states of mind such as creative blocks – have an amygdala (central to the brain's avoidance system) that is on high alert most of the time.[17] Once triggered, the avoidance system, as we know, compels you either to fight, freeze or flee. Although these reactions are normally sup-pressed in the workplace (often with some difficulty), they don't go away. They simply morph into other distressing thoughts, feelings and emotions. So, in practice, the 'fight' response can morph into a bad temper, the compulsion to 'flee' can turn into stress and depression, while the 'freeze' response can become a creative block that paralyses the mind and impedes rational thought. Whatever the initial response of the avoidance system, the end result is the same. The mind turns inwards and begins baiting itself. Before long, barbed self-critical thoughts rear their heads: *What's up with me today? Why don't I just get on with it? I've already spent hours on this and what have I got? I need to stop dithering and get a move on ... It's ridiculous! I used to be able to do things like this easily ... I must have a problem ...*

These harsh, nagging thoughts arise from your 'inner critic' – and they can be crippling.

JUDGING AND COMPLAINING

When your inner critic is in full flow it can sap your energy and enthusiasm for life. It can become impossible to think clearly or creatively. Rational solutions to problems become elusive. And the courage and determination needed to succeed can evaporate. In short, it undermines divergent thinking, which, as we know, is the type of thought that drives creativity. But while all of this is undoubtedly distressing, the inner critic has a far more insidious side – because even in 'normal' times the inner critic is still there, often just below the level of consciousness, judging and complaining in the background. It urges caution and guides you down the safest of roads (the inner critic hates uncharted territory). It seduces you into accepting the status quo and coaxes you into playing it safe, rather than pushing your creative boundaries. It tells you that nobody cares, that you are a cog in a machine and that it's best if you keep your head down in case anyone notices. This is because:

The inner critic is the voice of the negativity bias.

As Ilene Gregorian, a mindfulness trainer for US Special Forces, puts it: 'You can take yourself down with your thoughts faster than any enemy can ... Mindfulness will help you put a spam filter in your head.'[18]

INTUITIVELY RIGHT

When life becomes dominated by the negativity bias, when the inner critic is chipping away at your peace of mind and you feel trapped inside a creative black hole, it's tempting to try to think your way out of the problem and find a 'rational' solution. After all, such an approach has worked so many times in the past that it's tempting to give it one last heave; to break your creative block through sheer force of will and intellect. But this can often be the worst possible approach because it will simply trigger another round of habitual circular thoughts. It's like being trapped in quicksand; the more that you struggle to be free, the deeper you sink. What you need is a way of disengaging from the fight; of gaining perspective; of enhancing divergent thinking.

Trouble is, we have become so accustomed to *trying* to be creative and of *forcing* ourselves to solve problems by thinking our way through them that we've forgotten that there are other sources of inspiration. We have become so accustomed to thoughts acting as an intermediary between us and the world that we can forget that we are also *aware*. We can experience the world directly without thought acting as an intermediary – or a distorting lens. We have this magical property of consciousness. And it is this conscious awareness that is the key to unlocking creativity. Allow me to explain these nebulous and unorthodox ideas.

Rational thought, the inner critic, the negativity bias, convergent thinking and the autopilot are all features of the mind's *Doing mode*. Psychologists call it the Doing mode because it's very efficient at getting things done.[19] In essence, it works by solving problems incrementally – like this: you see yourself in a place (with a problem) and you know where you want to be (with a creative solution or a finished product). The mind then analyses the gap between the two and tries to bridge it. This fires up the mind's Doing mode, which breaks down the problem into smaller pieces, analysing each piece in turn and trying to solve it using rational, critical thinking. The mind then reassembles the pieces and reassesses the overall problem, to see whether the solution has got you any closer to your goal. The Doing mode is often fast and efficient. It frequently kicks in and solves problems without you even being aware of it. It's how we navigate, solve engineering problems and perfect everything from film scripts to computer software.

Main characteristics of the Doing and Being modes of mind

1. **Automatic pilot versus conscious choice:** the Doing mode is very efficient at automating your life by creating habits. This frees up time and cognitive capacity for other uses. The problem is that habits can begin to automate your entire life, so that you start to live inside your head, rather than in the real world. It can automate what you think, feel, sense and do. This erodes creativity. The Being mode, on the other hand, enhances creativity by cultivating full conscious awareness. This awareness allows you to see how much of your life is controlled by the autopilot and encourages you to break those habits that compel you to think along the same old lines. This opens the doors to chance, intuition, serendipity and to new ways of thinking and behaving.

2. **Analysing versus sensing:** the Doing mode analyses the world. It thinks, plans, remembers, compares, contrasts and judges. These are important skills, but they can backfire if taken to extremes. You can become hypercritical and find it difficult to make decisions. You can start to live inside your own thoughts and lose contact with the outside world. This can drive anxiety, stress, depression, insomnia and exhaustion. It also means that you are no longer paying full attention to the world and will fail to notice new ideas, concepts and information. So your view of the world will begin to fossilise. By contrast, the Being mode is a different way of knowing and 'understanding' the world. It puts you back into contact with your senses. It

dissolves the inner critic's running commentary on the world. It's more intuitive, sensory, 'fuzzy', lacks hard boundaries and is better at dealing with nuance and complexity. It's Wordsworth not Kraftwerk. It encourages you to make intuitive leaps and helps creative ideas rise above the background noise of your mind.

3. **Avoidance versus approaching:** the Doing mode works by holding on to your goals, but also by bearing in mind your 'anti-goals' – the things that you want to avoid. This can stimulate your threat-avoidance system and narrow your mind. It can make you feel wary, fearful and hypervigilant. Remember the mouse in the maze experiment and the negative effects of avoidance on creativity (see page 24)? By contrast, the Being mode is curious about the world. It loves novelty and urges you to approach, explore and embrace the unexpected. It is bold, playful, courageous and resilient to setbacks and 'failures'.

4. **Striving versus accepting:** the Doing mode compares the world with a version that exists only in your hopes, dreams, fears and nightmares. It focuses on the gaps between the two versions and strives to bridge it. The Being mode accepts the world as it is. This is not resignation to your fate, but rather a form of 'strategic acceptance': an acceptance of the situation as it is, right now. It's a period of allowing, of letting be, so that you can take stock of the situation. It is also an acceptance that things may soon change once again. This enhances your sense of perspective, broadens your mental horizons and thereby dissolves anxiety, stress and unhappiness. Such positive states of mind directly encourage your creativity to flourish.

5. **Viewing thoughts as 'solid' and 'real' versus seeing them as 'mental events':** the Doing mode uses thoughts and ideas as its currency. One thought builds on the next and the next. It builds ideas about the world and tests them in the mind's eye. This is a powerful way of solving problems, but your mind can begin to mistake them for reality. It can also create stress and a sense of tunnel vision that undermines creativity and drives procrastination. The Being mode creates a mental vantage point from which you learn that thoughts are just thoughts; they are passing mental events. At any given moment thoughts might be the product of your avoidance system, the negativity bias or perhaps be driven purely by habit. So they might be objectively true – or they might not. In either case, they are not 'you' or 'reality', but are, instead, the mind's running commentary on the world.

Balance

The Doing and Being modes are equally important. In the West, we have traditionally emphasised the Doing mode and allowed the Being mode to lie fallow. Mindfulness helps restore the balance by developing the Being mode and teaching you how to consciously switch between the two. If you can consciously switch between Doing and Being then you can approach ideas from contrasting directions. This is the essence of creativity.

The Doing mode is a tremendously powerful way of solving problems and is one of humanity's greatest skills, so it's only natural to use it whenever we face a problem. Trouble is, we use it so often that we have become unaware of its limitations. The Doing mode is very effective at solving problems where you can follow a logical train of thought (these are known as 'non-insight' problems). But it falls flat when a creative leap is required (for what are known as 'insight' problems). This is because the Doing mode becomes transfixed by the gap between where you are and where you want to be. When such a gap cannot be bridged through logic alone, in other words when it's an 'artistic' problem, or an insight problem that is simply too big, complex or nuanced to be solved consciously, then the mind begins to go around in habitual circles. It tries to bridge the gap using all of its normal problem-solving routines, but it simply cannot make the leap, resulting in ever more anger, stress and confusion. This fires up the avoidance system, which then pours more fuel on the flames and creates even more stress and fear, which further narrow the mind. So the mind can end up like an angry dog chasing its own tail.

To bridge such a gap you need to make a creative leap; to change mental gears. And you do this by harnessing an alternative way of relating to the world: the *Being mode*.[20] Psychologists call it the Being mode because it is a process that arises out of pure conscious awareness. It's when you are experiencing the world directly through your senses without thought acting as an intermediary. That is, when you are actually *experiencing* something first-hand, rather than thinking *about* it. It's like a mountaintop that is unclouded by thoughts, feelings and emotions. Or a vantage point that reveals how your mind can distort reality by overthinking, over-comparing and over-judging. It helps you step back from your thoughts and allows your mind to approach ideas and problems without any preconceptions – with a beginner's mind. Neuroscientists call it metacognitive awareness. And it's cultivated through mindfulness meditation.

The Being mode is no better or worse than the Doing mode, just different. It's more intuitive than thinking and can often be wiser too. The Doing mode only becomes a problem when it volunteers for a task that it cannot do, such as trying to solve problems where creative leaps are required, or trying to create a work of art or design where intuition is needed. Mindfulness meditation teaches you to recognise which mode your mind is operating in and this gives you the option of shifting mental gears. Sometimes it will be best to allow the Doing mode free rein to crunch through problems logically, rationally. At other times, the Being mode will be more appropriate. And the essence of creativity is nothing if not approaching the world from different angles in different states of mind.

If the Doing mode is convergent thinking, then the Being mode is divergent thinking.

For thousands of years people have learned how to cultivate the Being mode using mindfulness meditation. There is nothing mystical about any of this.

For mindfulness – or mindful awareness – simply arises out of this Being mode when you pay attention, on purpose, in the present moment, without judgment, to things as they actually are.[21]

Mindfulness allows you to see the world as it is. It allows you to tap into different ways of approaching the world that can help you to solve problems in radically new ways; to unearth new ideas; or to create great art, design or literature. And such a state of mind is only ever a single breath away.

CHAPTER THREE

The Creativity Programme

The next four chapters of this book are dedicated to the actual mindfulness programme. Each of them corresponds to one week of the programme, and each contains two elements. Firstly, there is the meditation programme itself, which takes ten to twenty minutes a day. The meditations can be downloaded from http://franticworld.com/creativity/

You will find detailed instructions for the meditations in the shaded boxes in each chapter, and when you actually carry out the programme it's a good idea to read through these first to familiarise yourself with them. However, it's best to carry out the meditations while listening to the audio tracks, rather than attempting to read instructions as you go along (or relying on memory).

Many people read through the whole book before starting the

programme. If you decide to do this, it's worth re-reading each chapter before you start on the corresponding week of the programme. Each week is built on many centuries of wisdom, so it helps if they are fresh in your mind.

The second element of the programme is the Habit Releasers, one of which should be carried out each week. Habit Releasers break down the negative habits of thinking and behaving that force you into approaching problems – and the world – in the same old unproductive ways, helping you to progressively 'jump the tracks' into new and more creative ways of thinking. They are generally interesting to do and require very little effort. Typical Habit Releasers include such things as going for a short walk in an area you've never been to before, visiting a seaside town or perhaps shopping in a different grocery store. You should aim to carry these out in an inquisitive and playful state of mind.

If you possibly can, carry out the meditations on six days out of seven. It does not matter which days you choose. The Habit Releasers can be performed on any day of the week. If you miss a day or two of meditation, don't worry. Simply make up the time on the other days by either meditating for longer or by doing the requisite number of extra sessions. You can then carry on with the next week of the programme. If you only manage to meditate on four days or fewer, then it's best to repeat that week. Mindfulness gains its power through repetition, so it is important that you do meditate on the recommended number of days. Life, however, can be busy, so it's not unusual to pause or stop for a while.

If you should stop meditating completely for more than a few weeks, it's preferable that you restart the programme. If this should happen, try not to criticise yourself. It's surprisingly common to make several 'false' starts, or to take breaks, when you start on any meditation programme. So instead of rebuking yourself, gently remind yourself that you cannot *fail* at meditation. The programme may, however, take longer to complete than you might wish. If this should happen to you, simply pick up the reins when you feel able. Making repeated false starts – or taking a long time to find a natural place for meditation in your life – can be valuable lessons in their own right. If you feel that you are not making as much progress as you might wish (or feel that you are not trying hard enough), then, once again, try to avoid criticising yourself. Learning to treat yourself with compassion and gaining an understanding of your own life are important elements of mindfulness. In their own ways, they also bolster courage and resilience.

The core *Mindfulness for a More Creative Life* programme in this book takes four weeks. However, you will probably find it so effective that you will want to continue meditating when the formal programme has finished. To help you do this, the final chapter of the book shows you how to build mindfulness into your life. You will also find extra Habit Releasers in the Appendix on pages 181–8.

Week-by-week summary of the programme

To enhance creativity and problem solving you need to cultivate three skills. Firstly, you need a calm, open and disciplined mind that can gather and integrate new ideas and information. Secondly, you need to notice the new ideas created by your mind and to realise their significance. And thirdly, you need the courage to follow your ideas wherever they should lead and the resilience to cope with the inevitable setbacks and criticism from others. Each of the first three weeks of the mindfulness programme focuses on one of these skills. The final week works on all three simultaneously. In practice, all of these skills are interconnected, so that if you work on one then you will also enhance the others.

Week One introduces the Breathing meditation. As the name suggests, this is a simple breath-based meditation that asks you to follow the sensations that the breath makes as it flows into and out of your body. This creates a sense of tranquillity that helps you to become more aware of your thoughts, feelings and emotions as they arise in your mind – and to let go of struggling with them. It teaches you to see your autopilot at work and to notice its tendency to drive repetitive (and frequently negative) patterns of thinking. These cloud the mind and hinder mental flexibility. You cannot get rid of the triggers for these negative mental habits, but you can change how you react to them. You can learn to let go of struggling with your more difficult thoughts and relate to them as you would clouds in the sky, watching them appear, drift past and disappear. This, in turn, encourages great clarity of mind and purpose. It also increases working memory capacity, so that you can more effectively gather information and deal with complex and rapidly changing situations. In short, it begins the process of enhancing divergent thinking. Focusing on the breath in this way has other benefits too: it slowly dissolves anxiety, stress and unhappiness by stimulating the parasympathetic or 'calming' aspect of the nervous system. This cultivates the soothing-and-contentment system and progressively rebalances the 'avoidance' and 'achievement' systems (see pages 23 and 15).

Week Two introduces the Sounds and Thoughts meditation. This enhances divergent thinking by teaching you to notice the similarities between sounds and thoughts. Both arrive seemingly from nowhere – you have no control over their arising nor their content; and both carry powerful messages that seemingly compel you into action. And just as we are bathed in a 'soundscape' of enormous depth and variety, we are immersed in a 'thoughtscape' of tremendous complexity. Understanding this similarity helps you to see that 'loud' habitual thoughts – just like sounds – are the 'noise' that clouds creative insight. If you can calm the mind, so that your thoughts are less habitual, then you can begin to 'hear' the quieter thoughts that often convey more subtle and creative ideas. This meditation also enhances mental agility by teaching you how to effortlessly shift the focus of your mind and style of thinking. In essence, you learn how to 'flick' between thoughts in the same way that you do with sounds. This greatly enhances flexibility and clarity of thought. The Sounds and Thoughts meditation enhances working memory too. And it also works on a deeper level by helping your subconscious mind to more effectively process information, reformulate problems and produce novel solutions and ideas.

Week Three builds on the previous two weeks with the Resilience meditation. This cultivates a broad, confident and kind-hearted state of mind that enhances courage and resilience. It creates a sense of perspective that allows you to respond to the world, rather than merely react to it. It does this by soothing your harsh inner critic and imbuing you with the courage necessary to follow your ideas wherever they should lead. Courage is essential for creativity to thrive. Such courage, combined with enhanced clarity of mind, will help you make and implement decisions more effectively. Because this meditation also enhances personal warmth, empathy and compassion it will begin to bolster your emotional and social intelligence. Such qualities are vital for effective teamwork, leadership and charisma.

Week Four introduces the Insight meditation. This enhances the three skills essential for creativity in one powerful meditation. It progressively dissolves negative ways of thinking, cultivates divergent thinking and fosters the courage and resilience necessary to succeed. It's the same flavour of awareness that has been cultivated for centuries by great writers, artists, creatives, philosophers, scientists and even business and military leaders.

A TIME AND A PLACE FOR MEDITATION

The meditations in this programme take only ten minutes and should be carried out twice a day. Slotting them in at the beginning and end of each day generally works well, but it is up to you when you do them. Early morning is often best for at least one session (shortly after breakfast but before leaving home is ideal). Other good times are immediately after returning from work or before your evening meal. If you plan to meditate shortly after returning home, you might like to have a small snack first. Even low-level hunger can be surprisingly distracting. And if you meditate in the early morning you may find that you have to get up and go to bed a little earlier, so that the practice isn't carried out at the expense of sleep. Regularity is important too as it cuts down on procrastination.

As the course progresses, you may like to make your sessions a little longer – perhaps doing two meditations in a row in the morning or evening (or you might like to continue after the meditation has formally ended). But make sure you keep practising for at least ten minutes at both ends of the day to maintain regularity.

There will be many times when you feel that you do not have any spare time to meditate. This is undoubtedly true. Life *is* busy and you do have many priorities to juggle. So if you did have any spare time, the chances are you would already have allocated it to something else by now. You will, therefore, have to *make* time to meditate. However, meditation tends to free up more time than it consumes because it helps to streamline life, so it will pay dividends. If you are still concerned by this commitment, ask yourself how much time you spend each day worrying, running through habits or procrastinating. Maybe you could promise yourself to devote part of this time to meditation. Some people are put off starting a mindfulness programme because they fear it might be seen as 'self-indulgent'. If this concerns you, then perhaps you could see it as a fitness programme for the mind. Many people spend several hours a week working out in the gym. Why not spend a little time doing the same thing for your mind?

It is best to meditate in a pleasant and peaceful place. This might be as simple as a tranquil corner of your home. Avoid the bedroom if you can because this might encourage drowsiness. However, if this is the quietest and most tranquil space, then it's OK to meditate there. It will be helpful to turn off the telephone, switch it to silent or divert it to voicemail, and you might also like to let others in your home know that you would like to remain undisturbed while you practise. Some people find this a little embarrassing, fearing that others will find mindfulness odd. More likely, however, is that your friends and family will be pleased that you are finding the time to enhance your life.

As for equipment: a laptop or a phone to listen to the meditation tracks, a chair to sit on and perhaps a blanket to keep your legs warm are all that you will need.

When you actually carry out the meditations try not to have a definite goal for them, such as trying to clear your mind of thoughts or aiming to achieve a state of calm tranquillity. These will arise quite naturally, but if you aim directly for them, you risk kick-starting the mind's Doing mode. This can end up triggering a cascade of plans, thoughts, judgments and comparisons that undermine the actual practice. So, instead, try – as far as you are able – to maintain a spirit of warmth, openness and playful curiosity. Be open to what you find. Do you remember the experiment involving the mouse in the maze puzzles from Chapter Two (see page 24)? This revealed that playful curiosity enhances creativity. It also dissolves the blockages that can trap you inside a mental cul-de-sac. Approaching your meditation sessions with openness, kindness, compassion and understanding will dramatically enhance their benefits. And over time you will learn that the spirit with which you approach meditation – and most other things in life – is often as important as the act itself.

As you progress through the programme, you will begin to find that many other benefits are beginning to accrue. You will probably find that any anxiety, stress, unhappiness or exhaustion that you may be feeling will begin to dissolve. You are also likely to begin to sleep more soundly and be quicker to laugh and slower to anger. So not only will you become increasingly creative and effective at work, but happier too.

HOW TO SIT

It is best to carry out the meditations while sitting on a straight-backed chair, ideally positioned facing outwards from a wall, so that you look out into the room. You should adopt an alert but dignified posture with your spine about 2–3cm from the back of the chair. This will leave your back free to follow its natural curves and create a sense of openness in the chest. It will also encourage alertness and emotional 'brightness'. The feet should be flat on the floor about hip-width apart. The hands are best left relaxed, with palms facing upwards, either on the lap or the thighs.

The best position is one that causes as little muscular strain as possible and encourages an attentive but relaxed state of mind. Whichever one you choose, remember that you will gain nothing by forcing yourself into a harsh or uncomfortable position. So if you have problems with your back, for example, you may prefer to carry out the meditations lying down or in another position that you find comfortable. But if you can, do carry them out while sitting in a chair. You certainly shouldn't feel the need to sit cross-legged on the floor. Newspapers and magazines love pictures of supple men and women meditating like this, but there really is no need to do so. Sitting cross-legged has nothing to do with the practice of meditation; it is simply the way people traditionally sat in the East, and while some people do meditate like this, it is often extremely uncomfortable.

You may need to shift positions part-way through a meditation. Again, this is not uncommon. Fidgeting is normal, and even experienced meditators need to move from time to time. If you do move, try to include that in your meditation, moving as mindfully as you can.

WHEN WILL YOU BEGIN?

How about now?

CHAPTER FOUR

Week One: Adapt

The doctor sat opposite the elderly Jewish lady and her daughter. He had some bad news. The blood drained from the old woman's face and she began scratching at her head once again. Both women looked desperately tired and worried. It was hardly surprising. A few months previously, Gussie had begun complaining of powerful headaches. Her family had eventually persuaded her to go to the doctor for a check-up but he could find nothing obviously wrong. Soon after, however, Gussie began telling her doctors about 'a snake crawling and wriggling' beneath her skull. The descriptions grew increasingly vivid and powerful as she was passed from one specialist to another. The doctors appeared to listen but paid little attention to what this old lady was *trying* to say. She spoke figuratively rather than factually, as befitted a lady from a different age and culture, so the doctors heard only the words, not the actual meaning behind them.

'They diagnosed senility,' says her granddaughter Ellen.[1] 'Senility comes with old age, after all, and makes people talk nonsense. When she grew more confused and unhappy they recommended electro-convulsive therapy – shock treatment, in other words – and asked my mother to give her approval.

'It was not until the autopsy was performed that they detected my grandmother's brain tumour.

'For years afterwards I kept thinking about the doctors' reactions to my grandmother's complaints, and about our reactions to the doctors. They went through the motions of diagnosis, but were not open to what they were hearing. They were not creatively exploring the symptoms and potential diagnoses. Mindsets about senility interfered. We did not question the doctors; our mindsets about experts interfered. We were all, in a sense, behaving "mindlessly".'

Ellen Langer, now a respected psychologist at Harvard University, and her grandmother were victims of everyday 'mindless' automatic behaviour. In Gussie's case, the doctors gathered the facts but failed to take account of the broader context that gave them meaning. So when they ran through the logical thought processes necessary to make a diagnosis they drew the wrong conclusions. The doctors' minds were hijacked by their autopilot, which ensured that they did their jobs unconsciously, without creative insight. They had done their job, but the patient had died.

The experiences of Ellen Langer and her grandmother illustrate what can happen when you try to solve a problem by mindlessly following your normal routines. And such mistakes are hardly unique to medicine. Wherever you look you will find examples of tired, old, habitual routines being used inappropriately to try to solve new problems. They lead to poor design, terrible business decisions, inept government and public administration and even air crashes and industrial accidents.

These things happen because habits are so incredibly seductive. They sneak up on us and guide our minds along comforting old tracks. In a sense, they put a transparent wall between us and the real world, so that we become spectators on our own lives, rather than truly living them. This is the antithesis of creativity. Creativity is, at its heart, about noticing and actively connecting with the world. It's about putting together disparate facts and concepts and then actively noticing the resulting new ideas and connections. And that is why the first step in this programme is designed to help you begin cultivating a clearer and more receptive mind that is open to new ideas and far less in thrall to the auto-pilot. This was traditionally done by spending a little time focusing on a normal routine activity such as eating or drinking while consciously noticing all of the flavours, textures and aromas. This teaches three important lessons. Firstly, it reveals just how much of daily life can slip by unnoticed when you aren't paying attention. Secondly, it teaches you to notice the gravitational pull of the auto-pilot as it seduces you into giving up conscious control of your life. And thirdly, it begins to reveal the differences between the Doing and Being modes of mind. That is, the difference between thinking *about* an experience and *experiencing* it first-hand.

In the past, a raisin was chosen as the focus of the meditation, but we shall use coffee. This is normally drunk (or gulped down) with almost no thought, so bringing full mindful awareness to it will reveal just how powerful the autopilot can be.

In many ways, the autopilot largely defines the whole experience of eating and drinking because so many flavours, textures and aromas are governed by unconscious expectation. But by bringing mindful awareness to the experience, you will discover the profound changes that can occur simply by slowing down and consciously focusing your attention on one single thing at a time, rather than mindlessly hopping from thought to thought.

The Coffee meditation[2]

Coffee and tea are drinks that are often taken for granted, which makes them ideal subjects for meditation. The aim here is to consciously pay full attention to a cup of coffee or tea as you drink it. Most people are surprised by the wealth of tastes and smells that normally pass over them completely unnoticed. Meditations such as this are used to reveal just how much of our sensory experience of life is governed by the autopilot – that is, you tend to experience what you expect to experience. It is also a good way of clearing and settling the mind before tackling an important project or decision. Repeat it whenever you wish, or do it with another type of drink. The same principle of bringing a fresh 'beginner's mind' to a routine activity can be applied to any aspect of daily life. And such a beginner's mind is one of the foundation stones of creativity.

1. If you are making the drink yourself, look closely at the coffee grounds (or tea leaves). Really observe them. Spend a few moments letting your eyes soak up every detail. Observe how the light bounces off the grounds or leaves. What can you smell?

2. Add the water. What can you hear? What can you smell? If you are buying your drink, soak up all of the sounds and smells of the café. Can you hear tinkling cups? The hiss of

water? The chatter of other customers? Try to tune directly into your senses, rather than mentally describing the experience in words.

3. If you are adding milk and sugar, watch how they dissolve. Does the smell change? Focus on the subtly different aromas.

4. Take a sip. Coffee has over thirty different flavours and tea has many more. See if you can sense some of them. Are there some bitter notes, sweet ones, sour ones? Is there a trace of treacly burntness?

5. Resist the temptation to gulp down that sip; instead, after a few moments, or when you feel that your taste buds have become saturated, swallow it. How does it feel? When you breathe in, how do your mouth and throat feel? Hot? Cold? Or hot followed by cold?

6. Repeat the previous two steps with another sip of your drink. Carry on repeating this for five minutes or until you've finished your drink. How do you feel? Is it different from normal? Did the drink taste better than if you had consumed it at your normal speed?

'So much taste'

The coffee meditation came as a shock to Jake. He normally drank coffee by the gallon and saw it as little more than raw fuel for his mind. It kicked his brain into gear in the morning and coffee breaks punctuated his day. But that didn't mean he tasted it; in fact, he barely noticed it at all.

'I didn't realise just how much taste coffee had,' said Jake. 'I thought that coffee tasted only of "coffee", but it has many more interleaved tastes. I was shocked by the intensity of its sweetness and bitterness, by the rich, burnt taste, and its under-lying sourness too. This meditation brought home to me just how much I'd been missing. I knew that I often did things on automatic pilot, but I didn't think that it governed what food and drink actually tasted like or that it had so much control over me. When I did this exercise, and noticed all of these com-plex tastes, it was like that moment on the motorway when you suddenly realise that you haven't been aware of driving for the previous thirty miles. That one cup made me realise that I hadn't been actually tasting coffee for years. I'd become so wrapped up in my own world that I'd lost contact with the real physical one.'

Jake's reaction to the coffee meditation is a common one. It can bring home to people that they've been missing out on substantial parts of their lives; that they haven't been experien-cing life to the full. Jake had been missing out on the countless tiny pleasures that mark the difference between a humdrum life and one that is truly pleasant, engaging and productive. You only ever have a moment to live – this one – and yet so few of us truly inhabit it. The past is a series of memories and the future has yet to happen. Jake knew this on a theoretical level, and yet the gravitational pull of his autopilot compelled him to live in the past – or the future – and only rarely in the present moment. This ensured that Jake was failing to live life to the full; it also meant that he had been failing to notice what was going on around him – and such noticing lies at the heart of creativity.

'It also struck me as a little odd that simply changing the way I observed an experience changed the nature of the experience itself. I don't want to get overly philosophical, but it made me question the relationship between myself and the experience. I've always believed that everything – including experiences – was objectively real, but that's clearly not the case. The way that you approach an experience, and the attitudes that you bring to it, affect the actual qualities of it.'

Halfway through the meditation, Beth realised that her daily coffee breaks weren't 'breaks' at all, but rather an opportunity for her mind to dwell on the feelings of anxiety and stress that lay just beneath the surface. 'As soon as I began to focus on the taste of the coffee I realised that my mind really didn't want to focus on anything at all. It was awash with random thoughts. I was thinking *about* the coffee and not really tasting it. My mind soon hopped off to worry about what other people in the office might be saying about me. I was worried that my clothes didn't project the right image and whether I should do my hair differently now that I'm no longer so young. I'm a director of a film post-production company, so these things do matter. I soon started worrying about my work, my lack of energy, the inability of our team to finish the edit we were working on and even what I was going to have for dinner. I was turning into a stressed-up worry machine. I just wanted everything to *stop* for a while so I could get a better grip on life.

'When I saw my mind behaving like this I realised that I really did need to get a grip before life became intolerable. I'd been thinking along similar lines for months, but this meditation brought it to a head.'

At first glance, the coffee meditation can seem a little inconsequential. How can drinking a single cup of coffee make any difference at all? It matters only because it reveals a deeper truth:

unless you consciously seize control of your autopilot, life will continue slipping through your fingers. This is the central tenet of mindfulness: relearning how to bring full conscious attention to everyday activities so that you can truly experience life in all of its bittersweet beauty. And to do this you will need to find a way of bringing this fresh 'coffee mind' to your whole day. You need to learn how to actively feel the 'tug' of the autopilot as it takes control of your mind so that you can, instead, make a choice to be more mindful. It is possible to do this because in the briefest of moments before the autopilot assumes control there is a pause, a gap, where choice exists. Mindfulness teaches you to recognise this gap so that you can take more considered action. It gives you a choice in how you react. You can opt to resume control over your life or to leave the reins in the hands of your autopilot. Sometimes it will be best to allow the autopilot to carry on its work. At other times you might wish to take full conscious control. You will, however, have a choice. You can learn to respond rather than react. And you do this through the daily practice of the Breathing meditation.

Practices for Week One

- Ten minutes of Breathing meditation (see page 65; track 1 on the download), to be carried out twice a day on at least six days out of the next seven.

- A Habit Releaser (see page 76).

BREATHING MEDITATION

The philosophers of ancient Greece believed that wisdom was imparted to mankind through the breath of the gods. Indeed, our own word *inspiration* means, literally, to breathe in. Mindfully focusing on the breath may not give you enlightenment from the gods, but it will certainly bring great clarity of mind. This, in turn, will allow you to observe the workings of your own mind, so that you can see how it unwittingly undermines creativity by tying itself in knots and muddying your thought processes. The Breathing meditation teaches you how to observe your thoughts – to look 'at' them, instead of seeing the world from 'inside' them – so that you experience the world directly, and not through a lens clouded by powerful emotions, preconceptions and irrationality. This is metacognitive awareness – an aspect of the Being mode – and it frees you from the autopilot that has mechanised so many of the negative thought patterns that are undermining your creativity.

The meditation works by inviting you to gently focus on the sensations the breath makes as it flows into and out of your lungs and to notice the effect this has on your whole body. Throughout the meditation, it is important to focus on the *sensations* of breathing, rather than the *idea* of breathing. Many meditators, initially at least, tend to think *about* the breath, instead of actually *experiencing* breathing first-hand. This is the key difference between the Doing and Being modes of mind.

Why is focusing on the breath in this way so important?

Firstly, it provides a dynamic anchor for your awareness. It allows you to sense when your attention has wandered and provides a focus to return to. This helps you to see when your mind has slipped into the circular, repetitive thought patterns that undermine creativity. You also come to a deep-seated realisation that your mind is in constant flux. It is never idle and thinks constantly. This is the Doing mode.

Secondly, it teaches you that you can relate to your thoughts in the same way that you do to the breath. Just as the breath rises and falls, thoughts ebb and flow. At any one moment these might reflect an accurate view of the world – or they might not. This can be a profound and liberating insight because you are no longer compelled to believe that your mind's running commentary on the world is completely true. You come to realise that it might, instead, be simply reflecting your emotional state driven by the body's regulatory systems; or perhaps running on autopilot, with your thoughts simply reflecting a habitual state of mind.

Thirdly, it helps strengthen your powers of concentration, so that you can effortlessly shift the focus of your awareness. See it as a form of exercise that gently builds and enhances your mental flexibility. This has positive ramifications across the whole of life.

Fourthly, it teaches you that the breath can become a sensitive emotional radar. All of your emotions are reflected in the breath. If you learn to focus on the breath while paying attention to your own emotional landscape, then you can begin to use it as a sensitive early-warning system. You can learn to sense when you are under pressure long before distressing thoughts appear in your conscious mind simply by becoming aware of disturbances in the normal rhythm of the breath. Such an alarm system allows you to defuse the 'negative' emotions that drive anxiety, stress, fear, anger and unhappiness before they gain unstoppable traction in the mind.

Fifthly, breathing itself can be profoundly relaxing. When you pay attention to the breath, and it becomes calmer, it naturally becomes deeper and more rhythmic. This stimulates the parasympathetic nervous system and is naturally calming.[3] So, paradoxically, noticing the build-up of negative emotions by the effect they have on your breath and body actually helps dissolve them. And actively 'breathing into' the areas of the body where the negative emotions appear to be localised can dissolve them even more effectively.

Throughout this meditation programme you will be asked to pay close attention to the sensations flowing through your body in the same way that you do with the breath. This is to help you understand the ways in which the body influences the trajectory of your thoughts, feelings and emotions. This happens because the mind does not exist in isolation; it is a fundamental part of the body and they both continuously share information with each other. In fact, many neuroscientists now believe that we think as much with the body as with the brain – that they should be seen as two complementary halves of the same system. It's called embodied cognition, and a good example of it is the way that the mind and body react to stress. The initial stress reaction might be triggered by something as subtle as an anxious memory flickering across the mind. The body will often detect such thoughts before we have even consciously registered them and frequently reacts as if they are tangible and real, whether they accurately reflect the world or not. So the first stirrings of stressful or anxious thoughts can cause the body to become slightly tense. The mind then detects these physical reactions and mentally braces itself for action. This mental bracing is then picked up by the body, which tenses even more. It's a vicious cycle where mental stress is reflected by the body as physical tension and such stress feeds back into the mind to drive anxious, stressful and depressing thoughts.

The whole process is phenomenally complex and full of positive and negative feedback loops, and scientists are only now getting to grips with its nuances and implications. Nevertheless, the influence of the body on the mind is surprisingly powerful. For example, research has shown that if you purposely stand tall, then not only will you feel more confident, but positive thoughts will begin flowing through your mind.[4] Physical sensations can alter your perception too. For example, in experiments people asked to squeeze something hard 'see' sexually ambiguous faces as male; when they squeeze something soft the same face is seen as female.[5] People who are forced to simulate a smile by holding a pencil between their teeth perceive jokes as funnier than those asked to purse their lips to simulate a frown.[6] And even humdrum physical sensations such as hunger, thirst or fatigue can exert a powerful effect over decision making. One study carried out by the Columbia Business School, New York, discovered that the chances of prisoners being granted parole were far higher after a judge had just eaten than if he was hungry (a 65 per cent chance versus virtually zero).[7]

So in practice, decisions can often be influenced at least as much by the state of the body as by any rational thought process. Mindfulness can begin to free you from this by helping you to become aware of the influence that the body has over thought, creativity and decision making. You can then begin to account for biases. You can also gain an alternative perspective on problems by learning to listen to your body: by, for example, paying credence to your 'gut reactions' and other sources of intuition. Such gut reactions are not 'mystical' in any sense, but simply represent the bodily manifestation of subconscious thought processes. You can also use this enhanced awareness to diffuse anxiety, stress and unhappiness before they gain unstoppable momentum. Such things can help you to respond rather than react.

Practicalities

The Breathing meditation takes only ten minutes and should be performed twice a day on six days out of the next seven. The best times are likely to be in the morning and evening, but it is up to you when you actually do them, although it is preferable to carry out the meditations at the same times each day. It is import-ant to establish a routine as this will support you on those days when your energy or enthusiasm is lacking. It's best if you read through the meditation guidance on pages 65–8 before actually doing it, and then carry it out while listening to the audio (track 1). It is also worth refreshing your mind about the practicalities of meditation (see pages 46–50). Choose, if you can, warm and quiet surroundings for your practice, and, unless you are listen-ing to the meditations on your phone, you will probably find it best if you switch it off or divert calls to voicemail. (If you are listening to it on your phone then set call and message alerts to silent.) You might also want to let others in your home know when you are meditating so they won't inadvertently disturb you.

When you begin the mindfulness programme it is quite likely that you will meet resistance. This is entirely normal. You might find that your mind suddenly discovers many new, more interest-ing or pressing matters to attend to. You might even feel a little shy or embarrassed about meditating; or perhaps you will start to feel guilty about devoting time to it. If this should happen, then remind yourself that this is *your* time that you have set aside to enhance your creativity and overall mental performance and well-being. This will not only benefit you, but all of those around you too. If resistance should still persist, then gently remind yourself of what others have found: *mindfulness tends to liberate more time than it consumes.* It does this by breaking down many of the habits of thinking and behaving that waste so much of the day – habits that force you to cover the same ground over and over again. As you become more aware of the workings of your mind and body, you will start to notice how much of your life is run by the autopilot. And when you do so, you will then have the option of stepping off the treadmill and using your time more creatively.

There may be times when you miss out on one of the meditations. If this should happen, try not to criticise yourself. Life can be busy, so it is not unusual for this to happen. If you should miss out on a whole day, then try and make up the time later in the week. If you should only manage to do the meditations on four days or fewer, then it's best if you restart the week. Bear in mind that it is not uncommon to make several 'false starts' on any meditation programme. Many people, including those who are considered to be accomplished meditators, made repeated attempts to build mindfulness into their lives. So try to remember this if you should manage to meditate only a few times over the next week. Each time you make a 'false start' you are actually learning a little more about how the mind works and how the autopilot can create resistance to mindfulness.

Breathing meditation

1. Sit upright in a straight-backed chair. Your spine should be allowed to adopt its natural shape in a relaxed but dignified posture about an inch from the back of the chair. Place your hands in your lap in whatever position feels the most comfortable. You can also do this meditation lying down, standing or even walking. The guidance assumes that you are sitting, but you can adapt the instructions as you go along to whatever posture you've chosen.

Checking in ...

2. Allow your body to settle down into gravity, letting it be held and supported by the chair beneath you.

3. Gently close your eyes. Begin by tuning into the world around you. It might be noisy inside or out. You might hear cars, wind, rain or human voices. Whatever is here, pay attention to the sounds for a moment. Try to remain receptive to them, rather than being drawn into them. Notice how they rise and fall. Try not to change anything. Simply listen to this constantly changing landscape of sounds for a few moments.

4. Gather up your awareness and focus your attention on your feet. Can you feel the floor beneath them? Do they feel warm or cold? Or perhaps tingly or a little achy? Pay attention to the sensations themselves. Consciously feel them, rather than think *about* them. Notice how the actual sensations rise and fall. If there are no sensations at all, then simply acknowledge this to yourself.

5. Now gently move your awareness through your whole body and feel the sensations in a similar way. How do your legs feel? Pause for a moment to soak up the sensations. Then slowly move your awareness to your pelvis, then your stomach and lower back ... your chest and upper back ... feel the rise and fall of the breath for a few moments.

6. And how do your arms feel? Move your awareness to your shoulders and pause for a few moments. Then move on to your neck and head. How do they feel?

7. Pause here for a minute or so while you soak up the sensations of your whole body. Feel its pulsating life as the different sensations rise and fall. Try not to change anything at all. Simply accept what you find.

The breath

8. Allow your awareness to gather around the sensations of the breath in your body. Where do you feel the breath most strongly? The stomach? Ribs? Shoulders? Nose? Or perhaps the throat? Be curious about the actual experience. Try to accept the experience for what it is, rather than having any expectations or judgments. Accept whatever you find.

9. Very gently rest your awareness within the whole torso. Can you feel your stomach rising on the in-breath and falling on the out-breath? Can you feel any movement and sensations in the sides of the body? In the back of the body? Try to bring a sense of kindly curiosity towards whatever you are experiencing as you breathe. Remember to accept whatever

is happening as you breathe. Become aware of the qualities of your breaths. Are they fast or slow? Shallow or laboured? Smooth or ragged? See if you can cultivate a precise awareness of the sensations and movement of the breath in the body as they happen, moment by moment, being careful not to force or strain any of them. In this way, follow the breath as it rocks and cradles the body for a couple of minutes.

10. From time to time your mind will wander. This is normal. Each time it happens, gently acknowledge where your mind went, then bring your awareness back to wherever the sensations of breathing are the strongest.

11. When your mind wanders again, as it surely will, become aware of any thoughts and emotions. As best you can, try not to criticise or judge them in any way. Try not to clear your mind of thoughts. Meditation isn't about having a blank or empty mind. It's normal to think. It's what minds do. So instead, can you look 'at' your thoughts and emotions, rather than 'from' them? Can you get a sense of being aware of what you are thinking and feeling without either blocking your experience on the one hand or getting lost or overwhelmed by it on the other?

12. Try to remember that thoughts are not facts – even those that claim to be. Can you let go of being caught up in them? Notice how they're continually changing one moment to the next in exactly the same way that your breath always changes. They're not as fixed and solid as you perhaps thought.

13. Each time that your mind becomes caught up 'inside' your thoughts and emotions gently acknowledge them by silently saying to yourself, 'Thinking, thinking', 'Worrying, worrying' or whatever feels most appropriate. Then return your attention to the rise and fall of the breath. Use it as an anchor for the mind over and over again. Follow the breath all the way in and all the way out. And each time your awareness wanders, as it will, simply note it and return to the breath – time after time after time. Be very kind and patient with yourself. Realising that your mind has wandered *is* the meditation. This is a magic moment of awareness: a moment when you've woken up from a distraction. So when you realise that your mind has wandered, you're succeeding in the practice, not failing; just as you are succeeding when you manage to stay with the breath.

14. Focus your awareness on the breath in this way for a few minutes more.

Checking out ...

15. Gently bring the meditation to a close. What sounds can you hear around you? Sounds near, sounds far. Are there any aromas? Can you feel anything unusual about your body? Stiffness, perhaps? Or the feel of clothes on your skin? Gently open your eyes and soak up whatever is in your line of sight. Gradually, gently, begin to move, making sure you give yourself time to make a smooth transition from the meditation to whatever you're doing next.

'I couldn't focus'

Did your mind become calm like a still pool during this exercise? Or did it chase off like a greyhound after a hare? Virtually everyone's mind becomes chaotic and unruly when they practise this meditation. Or rather, this appears to happen when in reality the technique simply reveals the mind's inner turmoil and innate desire to think at an ever-faster rate. Minds are designed to think, it's what they do, so it's not surprising that yours rampaged off in search of things to think about. Isobel learned this – countless times – during her first few Breathing meditation sessions: 'I was a bit surprised by how often and how completely my mind wandered. It was so seductive. One moment I was with the breath – and then I wasn't. I could never pin down precisely what had caused my mind to wander, but I'd get a sense of soft, gentle thoughts slowly crystallising in my mind. It was so gentle, so subtle, but irresistible. I'd gradually float away from the meditation. It was like falling asleep on a sunny summer's afternoon. After a while, I'd "come to" and realise that my mind had wandered. This was inevitably followed by a tremendous sense of failure *again*. I'd then have to bring my attention back to the breath. Shortly after, my mind would wander *again*. It was a nightmare, to be honest. I felt like a complete failure. I was hoping meditation would boost my concentration, but it seemed to be doing the opposite. I realised my mind was a bit of a mess. Focus seemed impossible.'

Iain encountered a similar problem. He knew he had a 'fast and crazy mind', as he put it, and 'one that put all kinds of ideas together', but Iain was none the less surprised by the speed with which his mind churned through thoughts. Before he had begun to meditate, he believed that this was a useful tool for generating new ideas, but the Breathing meditation revealed just how cha-otic his thoughts had become. His 'fast and crazy mind' was no longer a source of creative new ideas, but had instead begun to undermine them. This was largely because many of his ideas were circular and not new at all. So he ended up spending huge amounts of time attacking himself and his ideas. Such circular thoughts as *Why can't I just crack this?* or *Why do I waste so much time on stuff like this?* and *I'm losing it!* constantly washed through his mind. Such rumination was also undermining the very confidence he needed to snap out of the vicious cycle in which he found him-self. So with each twist of the cycle the energy and confidence he needed to escape his downward spiral were sapped even more. At first, he blamed the meditation for enhancing his turbulent thoughts, but it was, in fact, simply revealing the inner workings of his mind.

Both Isobel and Iain decided to persevere with the mindfulness programme after they were reminded that the aim of this medita-tion is *not* to still the mind, but to reveal its inner workings: to see how it ties itself in knots. Noticing that the mind has wandered and gently returning to the breath *is* the meditation. The state of mind it cultivates *is* mindfulness. The process begins as momen-tary glimpses – pauses almost – in the continual flow of thoughts across the mind.

Over the coming days and weeks these moments of mindfulness will lengthen and progressively join together into a more fluid state of mind that will begin to spill over into daily life. So your working memory will begin to improve and you will become increasingly focused and clear-sighted. This enhanced sense of perspective will dissolve any anxiety, stress or unhappiness that you may be feeling. In turn, this will leave you feeling happier, more centred and grounded. These psychological changes may be very subtle at first, but will gradually enhance your working memory and divergent thinking – the style of thinking that underpins creativity and effective decision making. It will also help rebuild the courage and resilience you need to follow wherever your ideas should lead. Such intrinsic confidence is central to creativity. It gives you the all-important *space* necessary for the natural flow of creativity to flourish.

When your mind wanders, you will probably feel annoyed. When it happens repeatedly you will likely want to force it back to focusing on the breath. You may start to attack yourself with bitter and barbed questions: *Why can't I do this? This is completely ridiculous – what's up with me today?* Try not to attack yourself though, as this will reinforce the habit of using force to think. As children we unwittingly learned to use mental force and barbed self-criticism to motivate ourselves, to keep to the track that adults had chosen for us. So we gradually forgot how to playfully explore the world. It was at this point that our innate curiosity and creativity began to wither. This habit will likely have worn very deep grooves in your mind and will probably be a difficult one to break, but this meditation will help you make a start. Rest assured that no matter how difficult it may at first appear, it will gradually become easier.

A central aim of this programme is to help you to stop attacking your ideas when they are first born. Creativity is a process not a product. You might think that many of your initial ideas lack merit, but some will lead to far more inspired ones. It is in the nature of creativity to produce half-formed ideas – which are then progressively fine-tuned. It's a process akin to sculpting. You begin with a formless idea and then, chip by chip, reveal what is inside. For this reason, when thoughts wander during meditation it's best, if you can, to bring a measure of kindness and curiosity to them. Numerous psychological studies have now shown that both are central to creativity. In practice, this is best done by paying attention to your thoughts for a few moments as soon as you realise that your mind has wandered. Be curious about them. Perhaps smile inwardly to yourself as a gentle acknowledgment that once again your mind has wandered and you have become aware of it. You might also like to say to yourself, 'thinking, thinking', 'anxious thoughts, anxious thoughts' or whatever feels most appropriate. Try not to criticise yourself. Remember that minds wander. And once you have acknowledged that your mind has wandered then return to the breath.

'I fidgeted all the way through'

Restlessness is another common difficulty faced during meditation. The mind does not like to be still, which is another reason why it conjures up circular thoughts. Fidgeting is another way in which it avoids stillness. There are other causes of restlessness too. The deep relaxation induced by meditation can, strange as it may seem, cause discomfort and even mild pain. This is because, as the body relaxes, all of the muscles, tendons and ligaments begin to return to their natural alignment, paradoxically, causing aches and pains. A good way of visualising this is to remember how it feels when you put down a heavy bag of shopping that you've been carrying for a while. First there is the release of unburdening yourself, but this is soon followed by aching as the muscles and tendons begin to return to their natural shape. Such realignments happen at different rates, so they tug and pull against each other, causing generalised aches and pains. After a while, everything has returned to normal and the pain dissolves. The same thing can happen in meditation, particularly if you have been stressed for some time.

There may be other unexpected drivers of restlessness too. Paul had serious problems with fidgeting during the Breathing meditation. After three days it suddenly dawned on him where the problem lay. As he relaxed into the meditation, two things were happening. He slumped very slightly and relaxed his stomach muscles, both of which caused his stomach to bulge out a little so that his belt and trousers bit into his waist and stomach. This, in turn, subtly altered his breathing. It became a little shallower and more laboured. As we saw earlier, there is an intimate connection between the breath and the autonomic nervous system and Paul's experience illustrates this perfectly. When the breath flows freely, the mind and body begin to relax; in turn, a relaxed mind and body encourage the breath to flow freely. It's a virtuous cycle.

But there is an opposing vicious cycle too. Restricting the breath causes the body to tense up and the mind senses this and becomes increasingly wary and stressed. This then restricts the breath and it becomes faster and shallower. So even the slightest restrictions to a free-flowing breath can feed back into the deepest reaches of the mind to create low-level stress and anxiety. And this is why Paul felt restless. The solution was as easy as undoing his belt a couple of notches and maintaining a more erect posture.

Remember in earlier chapters when I said that it was impossible to fail at meditation? Paul's experiences are a good example. When he realised that he was struggling, finding it impossible to stay focused, this was an important insight into his own mind's toings and froings. Equally, when he focused on the areas of his body that seemed to be giving rise to the restless sensations, and discovered that there was a straightforward physical cause, then that too was an important insight. Like Paul, you might find that if you have problems focusing, you will discover a simple cause. Often, a scattered mind can be caused by low-level hunger, thirst, tiredness, an ache or a pain or from sitting too long in an uncomfortable chair. The body is trying to tell you something, but the mind is simply not listening. So when you feel like this – whether you are meditating or not – spend a few moments reflecting on where the source of your irritation is located. Explore it. You may find that your restlessness results from something as simple as thirst or hunger.

'I felt a bit anxious'

If you have been under intense pressure to be creative or to make tough decisions, you might find that emotional tension rises to the surface during meditation. This usually takes the form of anxious, stressed or sad thoughts. You might be tempted to argue with these thoughts or emotions, to dismiss them or to try to ignore them. The most productive approach is to spend a little time watching them with the mind's eye and to feel the effect they have on the body. Be curious. You might find that stress is felt as tension in the neck, shoulders, jaw or hands. Anxiety might cause butterflies in the stomach. Sadness might manifest as tight or twitchy eyelids. A tear might appear. Emotions can arise as any number or variety of physical sensations. Wherever one appears in the body, simply pay attention to it. Try to remain with the emotion for a while. If you can, try to bring a measure of curiosity and empathy to it. After a while, you will begin to notice that such feelings soon pass. All emotions rise and fall. You might even begin to relate to these emotions like you do to the breath. Just like the breath, emotions are never static and unchanging. You might also like to try seeing them as shifting weather patterns. One moment you are in the midst of a powerful storm, but soon the clouds disappear and the sun might even come out. Whatever happens with the weather, the sky always remains. Your emotions are like the weather, but the awareness of your mind is as permanent as the sky.

Paying attention to your emotions in this way can transform suffering. To encourage the process you might like to name the emotions as you did earlier with your thoughts. You might acknowledge them as 'sadness, sadness', 'anger, anger' or whatever feels most appropriate. After you have done this, gently return your awareness to the breath. If these distressing emotions return repeatedly, you might try 'breathing into' them and feel them dissolve. You do this by focusing on the area of the body where they appear to be localised and then consciously feeling how the breath affects them as you breathe into and out of it. Even if the emotion is localised in a part of the body not normally affected by the breath, in practice you will find that most parts are touched by its subtle 'echo'.

'I fell asleep'

It's not uncommon to fall asleep during the Breathing meditation, especially if it is carried out while lying down. Many people see it as a sign of failure, but it is actually a sign of heightened awareness. If you have spent months or even years struggling with overwork then you may have got into the habit of not getting enough sleep. You will have 'learned' how to ignore the natural feelings of tiredness and developed the ability to soldier on through exhaustion. You may, in fact, have completely forgotten how to sleep soundly. But exhaustion is one of the biggest kill-ers of creativity and a major factor in poor decision making. The mind needs seven or more hours of sound sleep each night to function optimally. If it does not get it then it will begin to progressively shut down. If you fail to get sufficient sleep over a number of years, this lack may begin to inflict physical damage. Because mindfulness helps the mind and body to reconnect, any feelings of exhaustion will naturally bubble to the surface. So, if you fall asleep during your practice, congratulate yourself for catching up on some well-earned rest. It might also be a good idea to go to bed a little earlier until you have caught up on your sleep.

Meditation is simple

Most people, most of the time, do not struggle with mindfulness. The only reason for highlighting these potential issues is to give you the necessary preparation in the event that they do arise. Every difficulty you encounter is an opportunity to discover a little more about how your mind truly works and how you can harness its creative potential.

HABIT RELEASER: GO ON A CREATIVE DATE

A creative date is a block of time for you to nurture your inner spirit or creative flame. As the years pass, it's all too easy to forget the small things that used to make you happy and fed your soul. The pressures of life and work can erode life in myriad subtle ways. Think back to a time when you were half your current age. Were you more spontaneously creative? Were you ruled by serendipity? A creative date gives you the necessary time and space to rediscover this serendipity.

And what will you do? Anything at all. It can be a visit to a museum or art gallery or perhaps a trip to the cinema. You might like to go and see a car race, climb a mountain or swim in the sea. Or perhaps watch a sunrise or sunset, visit a castle, go to a music festival or learn how to be a fire-eater, a circus clown or how to ride a unicycle. Try to approach this Habit Releaser with a spirit of open-hearted playfulness. It's not just children who learn best through play – we all do. If you're short of ideas you can look at the Appendix (see pages 181–8) for inspiration. The essential aspect of a creative date is to simply do what you need to do to set your spirit free. So much of life is planned, ordered and hemmed in that it's important to throw caution to the wind and trust to luck. And when you do so, you'll find that your mind opens up to new possibilities – *creative* possibilities. Your senses will come alive once again and your spirit will be renewed.

Before you go any further, it's important to allocate the time for your date *now*. If you don't, it is likely to be squeezed out by other, seemingly more important, priorities. That's the nature of the autopilot, it tends to reassert itself. It's also important to defend this time against all comers. It's your time to spend as you wish. It should be for you alone. Don't feel the need to bring along friends, family members or your partner. If you feel guilty, gently remind yourself that this will be for everyone's benefit in the long run because it will help rekindle your innate creativity and love of life, without which your life and theirs are greatly diminished.

If you wish, you can make the creative date a regular feature of your life.

CHAPTER FIVE

Week Two: Create

A man and his son were involved in a car crash. The man died. The boy was rushed to hospital where the surgeon cried out: 'That is my son!'

Who is the surgeon?

Were you able to answer this question? Many people quickly come to an impasse. Your initial reaction was probably to say 'father' – but he is dead. This led down a blind alley that was surprisingly difficult to escape. You were probably left with such circular thoughts as *It's 'father'. No. Why isn't it 'father'? It must be … Was the boy adopted? Did the surgeon have an affair with the boy's mother? The surgeon must be the boy's father … I hate trick questions.*

If you haven't already worked it out (or heard the story before), the correct answer is 'mother', but few people get this without a flash of insight: an 'Aha!' moment.

This riddle is a classic *insight* problem; one that needs a flash of inspiration to solve.[1] Such conundrums reveal the way our mental biases can prevent us from seeing clearly into the heart of a problem. In this case, the lack of insight results from the concept of 'surgeon' being tightly linked to the idea of 'male'. So the word 'surgeon' automatically activates pathways in the brain associated with 'male'. This, in turn, biases the brain's search engines to look for answers with a masculine tinge. Female associations hardly get a look in because the mind is looking at the problem through male-tinted lenses. The reverse is also true. Other problems are looked at through female-tinted lenses, ethnic-, religious-, social-, political- or financial-tinted lenses ...

Our minds can become biased in countless other ways too. This is because we never experience an objectively real world; we do not see it in photographic detail. Instead, our minds try to make sense of things by constructing a model of reality that is constantly updated to take account of new and endlessly changing information. Manipulating our internal 'reality model' is the way we commonly solve problems, conjure up new ideas and plan for the future. Trouble is, we are often forced to make sense of the world with incomplete and confusing information. So we have to make inferences from the best available 'facts'. The mind judges these, integrates them with past experiences, extrapolates them into the future and attaches emotional meaning to them. And each time it does so, the model is updated and the whole cycle begins again. We do this every moment of every day – even while asleep. It is only when we come across an insight problem that we become conscious of just how perplexing the whole process can be. For this reveals that many of our interpretations about the world are actually driven by expectation, emotion and the autopilot, rather than representing a 100 per cent accurate picture of reality. These interpretations can force us to think in circles, in clichés – and if this should happen, it can ensure that we fail to have a true insight into the nature of the problem that we are looking at. So we end up approaching it with a mind that is clouded by thoughts *about* the problem, instead of gaining a clear insight into its true nature; we become trapped by the problem itself, rather than being liberated by finding elegant solutions to it.

Strange as it may seem, many of the qualities we normally associate with intelligence actually impede the solving of insight problems.[2] While we often praise logic, memory, eloquence and expert knowledge, they are all prone to bias because they rely on language to manipulate concepts in the mind. In technical parlance, we can become locked into 'verbal-conceptual' thinking. A good example is expert knowledge. In the previous chapter we saw how Dr Ellen Langer's grandmother was misdiagnosed with dementia through the 'mindless' application of expert knowledge. And this process of becoming blinded by experience can set in surprisingly quickly. In 2012, Israeli psychologists Jonathan Greenberg, Keren Reiner and Nachshon Meiran investigated this effect in a series of revealing experiments.[3] They asked a group of students to measure out a precise volume of water using three jars of different sizes. For example, in one experiment they were asked to measure out 100 units of water using three jars: jar A held 21 units of water, jar B held 127 units and jar C held 3 units. So, to measure out 100 units, the students had to fill jar B and then pour out enough water to fill jar A once and jar C twice. The students were then asked to measure out amounts of water using jugs of different sizes. Crucially though (and unbeknown to the students), all of the volumes of water requested by the experimenters could be measured out using the same formula – that is, by filling up jar B and then pouring out enough water to fill jar A once and jar C twice. Although the students found the problems quite difficult at first, they soon got the hang of it and busily ploughed through them. This meant that they very quickly built up expert knowledge about the task. But this being a psychology experiment, there was more to it than met the eye. After the students had learned the routine for solving the problems, the psychologists slipped in some other ones that could be solved by a simpler formula. Although these new problems were significantly easier, the students were completely oblivious to the simpler solutions that were right under their noses, and so they carried on using the original formula.

Although the students didn't realise it, the scientists were using these experiments to measure their 'cognitive rigidity' – that is, their ability to adapt to new circumstances and to think of ways around a problem. It turned out that after just a few minutes of practice, the students' minds had begun to fossilise and close down. They were blinded by their own experience and incapable of 'seeing' simple and elegant solutions that were right before their eyes. And experience is the Doing mode writ large.

The researchers then repeated these experiments with students who had been taught mindfulness. It turned out that their cognitive rigidity scores were more than a third lower than those of the students who hadn't been taught to meditate. Mindfulness had helped the students to 'de-bias' their minds, which became more flexible and better at generating new ideas. In other words, they had become more creative. And this creativity arose as a moment of insight (an 'Aha!' moment) that allowed them to come up with a solution that was independent of the thoughts that surrounded the problem. They were able to step outside the confines of the problem – to jump the tracks – so that they didn't get bogged down in the detail. In essence, mindfulness allowed them to spontaneously restructure the problem, and when they did so, the answer appeared in their minds. It was the Being mode writ large.

The researchers concluded that 'mindfulness meditation reduces cognitive rigidity via the tendency to be "blinded" by experience' and that meditators are more likely to 'identify the simple novel solution' to a problem.[4]

Experiments show that mindfulness not only reduces the tendency to be blinded by experience, but actively promotes creativity as well. In 2012 scientists at the University of Groningen in the Netherlands discovered that a specific type of mindfulness, known as 'open-monitoring' meditation, enhances insight problem solving – that is, seeing and solving problems in a novel way.[5] In other experiments they discovered that meditators were far better than non-meditators at solving the insight problem of the surgeon and her son told at the start of this chapter.[6] Another landmark study, undertaken at Leiden University in the Netherlands, discovered that open-monitoring meditation promoted divergent thinking, the type of thinking that helps to generate new ideas and underpins great art, design, science and engineering.[7] Nor do you need to spend months or years meditating to gain these benefits. According to research, just four days of daily practice can significantly enhance working memory and clarity of thought.[8] Other studies suggest that the benefits arise immediately after a meditation session.[9]

Numerous studies have now shown that mindfulness gradually rewires the brain, and you will begin to feel the benefit of this as you proceed through the course.[10] So, with practice, you will become increasingly creative and more adept at problem solving.

Practices for Week Two

- Ten minutes of Breathing meditation (see pages 65–8; track 1 of the download), to be carried out once a day.

- Ten minutes of Sounds and Thoughts meditation (see pages 90–3; track 2 of the download), to be carried out once a day.

- A 90-Second Breathing Space meditation (see pages 101–2; track 3 of the download), to be carried out at least once a day.

- A Habit Releaser (see pages 102–6).

THE QUIET VOICE INSIDE

Week One of the mindfulness programme helped you to begin training your mind so that you could focus more easily. This is the bedrock of mindfulness. Learning to focus can be a slow process and is often quite frustrating. You probably found that your mind repeatedly wandered. As explained previously, this is entirely normal – minds wander. You will have also learned just how much the mind chatters. Once again, this is not unusual. It is tempting to believe that these thoughts offer an unerringly accurate picture of the world, but often they do not. The mind uses thoughts to weave a coherent narrative out of a complex world – so they are often its running commentary on the world and, as such, they frequently represent no more than an educated best guess about what's going on.

Noticing that your mind wanders, and that it chatters, can be an important insight into its machinations, and this will have begun to reveal just how much of your behaviour and how many of your thoughts, feelings and emotions are driven by the autopilot. This metacognitive awareness (see page 39) – or noticing your thoughts from the 'outside' – is of profound importance because it helps you to realise that you are not your thoughts. They are one aspect of you – but they are not *you*. You are so much more than the mind's running commentary, and this realisation will ultimately give you far greater control over your life, which, in turn, will begin to dissolve any anxiety, stress or unhappiness that you may be feeling.

Although you may not be aware of it just yet, your mind's running commentary will have already become a little quieter and less frenetic. Moments of calmness will have become more frequent and tended to last a little longer. Your field of awareness will also have broadened somewhat. These are all signs that your mind is rebalancing itself so that the Doing and Being modes can work in greater harmony. Ultimately, this will enhance creativity and insight problem solving in two ways. Firstly, when the mind becomes a little calmer it allows your quieter and more creative voice to rise above the background noise. Secondly, broadening awareness enhances working memory and gives you greater insight into the world around you. This increases the likelihood of putting ideas together and having a moment of creative insight.

In Week Two of the programme we will take these concepts a little further with the Sounds and Thoughts meditation.[11] This will give you a first taste of an 'open-monitoring' meditation that will progressively boost creativity and clarity of thought. You will probably also begin to notice some welcome side-effects: any anxiety, stress, depression or exhaustion that you may be feeling will dissolve bit by bit. And these benefits will continue to accrue over the coming weeks in tandem with your enhanced creativity.

THE SOUNDS AND THOUGHTS MEDITATION

As the name suggests, the Sounds and Thoughts meditation reveals the similarities between sounds and thoughts. It teaches you that you can relate to your thoughts in the same way that you do to sounds. Both arrive seemingly from nowhere. You have no control over their arising or their content. Both carry powerful messages that seemingly compel you into action. In a sense, just as the ear is the organ that receives sounds, the mind is the organ that perceives thoughts. And once you grasp this similarity you can begin to see that 'loud', insistent, habitual thoughts – like sounds – are the 'noise' that clouds creative insight. If you can soothe the mind, so that your thoughts are less habitual, frenetic and fevered, then you can begin to 'hear' the quieter thoughts that often convey deeper and more creative insights.

Once again, it's important to emphasise that there is nothing wrong with thinking. The aim of mindfulness is not to *stop* the mind from thinking (if such a thing were possible), but simply to become *aware* of thinking and the way the mind works. Once you understand this at a deep and visceral level, then your thoughts can be seen for what they are: as guides, as works in progress and as sources of inspiration, rather than absolutely true pictures of the world. And when you can do this, your noisiest and most fevered thoughts will begin running into the sand, leaving behind a calm, clear and insightful mind.

The Sounds and Thoughts meditation works on many levels simultaneously:

- Firstly, it calms the mind so that your quieter and more creative voice can rise above the background noise.

- Secondly, by teaching you to pay attention to your thoughts, it gradually enables you to notice novel and interesting thoughts and ideas as soon as they arise.

- Thirdly, it teaches you how to effortlessly shift the focus of your awareness and style of thinking. In essence, you learn how to 'flick' between thoughts in the same way that you do with sounds. It's analogous to the 'cocktail-party effect', whereby you can hear your name mentioned by a person on the other side of a noisy room even though the volume of their voice is well below that of the general background hubbub. Being able to shift the focus of your awareness in this way greatly enhances mental flexibility and clarity of thought.

- Fourthly, it enhances working memory and puts problems in context by increasing the depth and breadth of your awareness. This weakens the hold that habitual thought patterns, emotions and associations have over you.

- Fifthly, it allows your deep subconscious to more effectively process information, reformulate problems, capture the essence of an idea and conjure up solutions.

Taken together, these benefits increase the chances of putting ideas together and having a moment of creative insight. This, in turn, creates clarity and subtlety of thought, while also dissolving any anxiety, stress and unhappiness that you may be feeling.

The Sounds and Thoughts meditation has two elements to it – they are receiving and noticing.

Receiving

In this, you receive sounds as they come – and then go. You see the body as a living microphone that receives sounds as waves in the air. You tune into each sound with its own volume, tone, pitch, timbre, pattern and duration. In the same way, you move on to 'receiving' thoughts and any emotions that they carry. You see the moment that they arrive, notice how long they stay and the moment that they dissolve.

Noticing

In this, you notice the layers of meaning that you add to the experience of the sounds. You might find that you label them, pursue those that you like and push away those that you dislike. The aim is to notice when you first react to the sounds and then return to receiving them. In the same way, you move on to noticing thoughts and feelings as they arise, the associations and stories they trigger, and the way that they entice you into their drama.

Practicalities

This week there are two main meditations to carry out. The first is the Breathing meditation (see pages 65–8; track 1 of the download). This is identical to the one you did last week. The second is the Sounds and Thoughts meditation (see pages 90–3; track 2 of the download). Each takes ten minutes. It is best to carry out both of this week's meditations on six days out of the next seven, and at different times of the day. It's entirely up to you when you do them, although most people tend to do the Breathing meditation in the morning and the Sounds and Thoughts meditation in the evening.

The Breathing meditation should ideally be carried out in warm and quiet surroundings, so remember to arrange not to be disturbed. The Sounds and Thoughts meditation relies on a little low-level background noise, so it's better to do it outside if you can. A garden, balcony or park would be perfect – but do remember to wrap up warm if it's cold so that you are not distracted by the temperature. If you are doing this meditation at home, it might be worth opening a window to let some sound in.

It's a good idea to refresh your mind about the general practicalities of meditation (see pages 46–50) before you start, and to read the guidance for both meditations (see pages 65 and 90) to familiarise yourself with the techniques. As with last week, you should listen to the audio tracks while you actually carry out the meditations. This week you might also like to extend the meditations by sitting quietly for a while after the tracks have finished. Many people do this quite naturally. Another option is to do an additional Breathing meditation immediately prior to the Sounds and Thoughts one. If you do this, make sure that the combined meditation is just one of your daily sessions. This increases the effectiveness of the whole programme, but it is up to you whether you do it or not. You might like to create a playlist to make this a little easier.

Sounds and Thoughts meditation[12]

If you are doing this meditation at home or at work, then it is preferable to sit upright in a straight-backed chair. If you are doing it in a public place, find somewhere to sit where you are upright and your back is self-supporting. A park bench is ideal. You can also adapt this meditation and carry it out on buses, trains or aircraft.

1. Begin by gently closing your eyes. Spend a few moments allowing your head, neck and shoulders to relax.

2. Gather up your awareness and begin to focus on the movements of the breath in your body. When you feel settled, gradually expand your awareness to include your whole body. Can you sense your whole body breathing? Spend a minute or so focusing on the movements of the breath in the body as if you were practising the Breathing meditation.

Sounds

3. Expand your awareness to include any sounds that surround you. Be open to them. There is no need to actively seek them out. As best you can, simply be open and receptive to them as they arrive. You might notice the sound of a television, air-conditioning, music or perhaps people talking. You might hear cars, trains or aircraft in the distance, or perhaps the sound of wind, rain or birdsong. The 'soundscape' has enormous depth and variety. Become aware of whatever is here.

4. Notice as the sounds arrive from all directions: from the front or back, above or below, from the left or right, sounds near, sounds far. See if you can sense their arrival, how they linger, and then slowly fade away. You have no control over their arrival or departure, or how long they stay.

5. As best you can, be aware of sounds as sounds, as raw sensations. Notice the tendency to label sounds such as 'car', 'wind' or 'siren'. See if it is possible to notice this labelling, and then to refocus your awareness on the sounds themselves, on the raw sensations.

6. Pay attention to the qualities of the sounds: to the way they rise and fall, to their pitch and timbre. See if you can notice how the louder or more obvious sounds tend to 'crowd out' the quieter ones.

7. Notice the gaps between the sounds. Can you gain a sense of the silence? You might notice that this silence is relative. Even silence may contain very subtle, quiet sounds on the edge of hearing. If you are in a very quiet place, you might be able to hear your breath, your heart or perhaps the rush of blood through your inner ears. Be open to them all.

8. As best you can, try to avoid becoming drawn into any individual sounds. You might find yourself thinking *about* sounds. When this happens, simply acknowledge where your mind has wandered to, and gently bring your awareness back to the sounds as they rise and pass away.

9. Focus your awareness on the soundscape in this way for three or four minutes.

Thoughts

10. Gently shift the focus of your awareness to your thoughts. Notice how thoughts arise in the mind, linger for a while and then dissolve. Just as with sounds, you have no control over their arriving or leaving, so there is no need to try to make thoughts come or go. Just as with sounds, you cannot control the type or intensity of thoughts flowing across your mind. All you can do is be aware of them. As best you can, see thoughts as events in the mind. See if you can relate to them in the same way that you do to sounds.

11. Thoughts can be likened to clouds in the sky. Sometimes they are dark and stormy; at other times they may be soft and wispy. Sometimes they fill the entire sky, while at others they dissolve completely, leaving it clear and empty.

12. If powerfully charged thoughts or emotions should arise, pay kindly attention to them, and allow them to be just as they are. Just like sounds – or clouds in the sky – they will eventually change or disappear completely.

13. If you should begin to feel lost in your thoughts, as if your mind has become unfocused and scattered, then gently bring the focus of your awareness back to the breath. Feel the sensations of breathing for three or four breaths, then gently return to the thoughts flowing across your mind.

14. In this way, continue paying attention to your thoughts for three or four minutes.

15. Gently bring this meditation to a close. What can you

hear? What can you smell? What can you feel on your skin? Sunlight perhaps? Or maybe the wind? Or perhaps clothes on your skin? Gently open your eyes and soak up whatever is in your line of sight. Gradually, gently, begin to move, making sure you give yourself enough time to make a smooth transition from the meditation to whatever you're doing next.

'I went to the park'

Matt struggled with the Sounds and Thoughts meditation. At first, he used his normal quiet spot at home for it, but somehow this felt a little sterile. It was too quiet for him, so he repeated the meditation a few hours later while sitting on a park bench overlooking the city. He could hear children playing in the distance, the occasional dog barking, birds singing, and every few minutes a train would slowly trundle past. So there was sufficient noise for his mind to focus on, but enough moments of silence too.

'This time the "sounds" part of the meditation went well,' said Matt. 'I can only describe it as "delicious". The "soundscape" of our park has the most wonderful texture. I was able to maintain my focus on the sounds and notice their variety, depth and the way that they rose and fell. I was able to be the observer without becoming wrapped up in the sounds.

'When I shifted the focus away from the sounds and towards my own thoughts it became far more difficult. It was both fascinating and frustrating. I found that my mind simply would not focus for more than a few seconds at a time. I spent the first two or three sessions wrestling with my mind, even though, deep down, I knew that I should not fight my thoughts or try to suppress them in any way. I knew that I should simply accept the turbulence in my mind and watch all of its toings and froings, but I simply couldn't.'

Matt then decided to bring a sense of playful curiosity to his observations. Instead of being the cold and steely observer, he adopted the attitude of the children he could hear in the distant playground. 'Kids are curious about everything,' he said. 'Nothing throws them at all. If something is difficult, and they fail at it, they simply pay a little more attention to it and have another go. So that's what I decided to do.'

When he brought this spirit of playful attention to his thoughts, he found their ebb and flow across his mind captivating. First, there was an initial 'spark' – an individual thought – that appeared in his conscious mind, seemingly from nowhere. It often arrived fully formed and usually took the guise of a mental picture. It was almost frozen in time, as if it were a single concept akin to a single frame of a film. This frame soon began to fade and was replaced by a ripple of feelings and emotional associations that spread outwards from the original thought. These ripples triggered more thoughts. Very soon, the conscious mind began to weave together these individual thoughts into a 'story' that felt very real and compelling. It was as if the individual pictures were being assembled into a reel of film that his mind was playing back to itself. And this stream of thoughts carried a huge emotional punch that at first seduced him into following the storyline, but then very quickly forced him to continue watching the 'film' in his mind. Thus, Matt began to sense two layers of consciousness: the first consisted of individual thoughts; the second was the story that the mind created from them. Matt noticed that most of these thoughts and feelings and the resulting storylines were very familiar. Then he realised why: they were being triggered by habit. These habitual thoughts were mostly worries about his job as an advertising photographer. His work had been drying up of late and it had been playing on his mind, so it was hardly surprising that thoughts cropped up such as *I haven't got time to meditate today, I need to sort out my portfolio, Oh God, I hope the shoot goes OK tomorrow, I really can't face the editing* . . .

'I then began to realise just how many of my thoughts were circular, self-defeating and habitual,' said Matt. 'It wasn't just the negative thoughts either. It suddenly dawned on me that the reason that I hadn't been coming up with new ideas for my fashion shoots was because I'd settled into safe and predictable patterns. This ensured that even when I'd tried to shake things up a little, it meant that I'd actually been trying to do things differently in the same safe and predictable way. I'd tried all of the usual tricks of my trade to come up with new ideas, but they'd failed because it was still me who was doing the trying. So I needed to change my approach – change my mindset. Understanding how my mind led me down the same tracks over and over again was a great help. It meant that I could consciously see when I was heading down the usual creative cul-de-sac, and this meant I could then choose a different route. It didn't help with the shoot the next day . . . that was probably too much to ask . . . but it helped with later ones.

'This meditation allowed me to see that these habitual thoughts were "noise" that was obscuring the more interesting ones hiding in the background. The odd thing was, when I did focus on the "noisier" habitual thoughts, they really did dissolve. It was almost as if paying attention robbed them of momentum. They "froze", and without momentum they simply melted away. I began to see my thoughts as messages. By observing each individual thought I was, in a sense, accepting their message, so they'd done their job and simply evaporated. This meant that my mind became far calmer and clearer. I felt less "jangly" inside and was able to focus more.

'I began to develop a sense that my mind – or field of awareness – was gradually becoming broader and able to handle more ideas at once. This meant that when I was planning a shoot, or on location or editing, I was more intuitive and open to new ideas. I could sense my intuition more keenly and had the confidence to follow where it led. I'd often not know where my intuition was leading me, but I could feel in my bones that I was moving in the right direction. And it worked. In a sense it helped me to rediscover my old way of working, which was built around gut instinct and intuition. This had made me a very successful photographer, but somehow that very success brought boredom and "sameness" to my photos. So it was great to go back to the source of my intuition – and realise that it was still there.'

'I felt angry, then sad'

There is a fine line between taking a curious and playful interest in your thoughts – and becoming seduced by them. Ruth repeatedly found herself becoming embroiled in her thoughts. She found that her mind had become a cauldron of sad and bitter thoughts about her seeming inability to get on with her job as a creative at a social-media marketing agency. These thoughts came to a head a couple of days into Week Two of the programme.

'I'd been having quite a few problems at work with an awkward boss, so it was difficult for me to get into the compassionate spirit of meditation. I'm quite forthright – some might say combative – so my instinct is always to come out fighting. When I began to meditate, I found that I kept getting dragged along by my thoughts. I found that as soon as my mind cleared, and I relaxed a little, a thought would pop into my mind that I'd find impossible to ignore. Often I'd become angry. Before I knew it, my head would be filled with plans to get even with my bosses, and then I'd feel guilty when I remembered that I was supposed to be meditating, not planning the downfall of the company. I kept on finding myself veering between anger and feelings of guilt [for feeling angry], and then a deep sadness would set in. Meditation did not seem to be helping.'

It's not unusual for people to feel emotional during meditation. This happens because when the mind clears and begins to calm down, you become more aware of the individual thoughts, feelings and emotions washing through you. Mindfulness reveals your thoughts and emotions – it does not create them. This is especially true if you have been under a lot of pressure. All of your thoughts can suddenly rush to the surface as soon as the pressure is released. It's akin to opening a bottle of pop or beer. So Ruth's experiences were not unusual. She was simply becoming more aware of the way her thoughts bounced off each other and fed a vicious cycle of anger, bitterness and guilt.

If you should find yourself filled with emotionally charged thoughts, the answer is to accept them without judgment, as far as you are able. As Matt discovered, this saps a vicious cycle of its momentum. Your thoughts are akin to propaganda. They may be true, or they might not. When you are looking from the perspective of your thoughts (from 'inside' them) it is impossible to say how accurate they are. So when you find yourself in this position, it is best to gently acknowledge the presence of your thoughts by perhaps saying to yourself, 'Thinking, thinking' and then return the focus of your awareness to the breath for a few moments, picking up the meditation where you left off. You could try seeing this as strategic acceptance. You are simply accepting the situation as it is – for now. So there is no need to rush in and try to put things right.

'I found it very difficult to maintain my mindful awareness for more than ten or twenty seconds,' said Ruth. 'But I eventually came to an acceptance of that – and when I did so, I found that I'd notice when my mind had wandered off far more quickly. Instead of it taking a minute or two for me to realise I'd been sucked in by my thoughts, I began to notice after maybe thirty seconds. I remembered my meditation teacher saying that an accomplished meditator is not one whose mind does not wander, but one who becomes very used to beginning again.

'So now I've accepted that my mind wanders during meditation – often quite a bit. But this is who I am. I'm a fireball. I get angry and sad. But that doesn't matter. I now get on with my job with full acceptance of who I am, with all of my faults and failings. Instead of battling myself, and those around me, I've learned to tune into my emotional peaks and troughs with the help of mindfulness. Some days I use my fiery energy to drive a project forward. Other days, when I'm on more of an even keel, I focus on the work that needs a little more insight. Now that I'm no longer so wrapped up inside the drama of life, I'm far happier.'

Understanding your own mind – and how it unwittingly ties itself in knots – is one of the central skills of mindfulness. At its core, mindfulness is about accepting that we are neither perfect nor all-knowing creatures. Our minds can often be noisy and irrational places. But, in the quiet spaces in between, can lie moments of piercing insight.

THE 90-SECOND BREATHING SPACE

By now you may have begun to realise one of the great ironies of meditation: as soon as it begins to improve your life, you can lose the incentive to continue. When you're in the midst of creative flow, or when life is fun and productive, it's difficult to see why you should meditate. You will also have learned one of the other great ironies of meditation – that mindfulness tends to evaporate when you need it the most: when you're struggling with a problem, you just want the inspiration to conjure up a solution; when you're angry, bitter or stressed, you just want to bulldoze your way through all comers; and when you're anxious or depressed, you can't seem to find the motivation to meditate.

The 90-Second Breathing Space was created for times such as these. It is a mini-meditation that serves as a bridge between the longer and more formal practices and the demands of everyday life. It allows you to regularly 'check in' with yourself and to nudge your mind in a more creative direction. It helps you regain a sense of being 'grounded' with warmth, kindness and safety. Many people say that it's one of the most important skills they learn on their mindfulness course.

The meditation has three main benefits. Firstly, it's a means of punctuating the day with mini-meditations to help you maintain a more creative state of mind. Secondly, it helps to defuse negative states of mind before they can gather unstoppable momentum. And thirdly, it's an emergency meditation that you can carry out in times of acute anxiety, stress, unhappiness, anger or exhaustion.

The technique consists of three stages of roughly 30 seconds each. In effect, it condenses the main elements of the whole mindfulness programme into a minute and a half. A good way of viewing it is to imagine your awareness moving through an hourglass shape as the meditation progresses. At first, you are asked to become fully aware of the thoughts flowing through your mind and the sensations in your body in a broad and holistic sense. You then gather up and focus your awareness on the sensations of the breath as it flows into and out of your body. And finally, you expand your attention outwards again, to encompass your whole body and to imbue what you find with warmth and compassion. You then expand your awareness even further to fully re-engage with the world.

The meditation should be carried out at least once each day (and preferably twice) and it is entirely up to you when you do it. You can do it anywhere you choose: on buses, trains, in the office, a café, the park or even on the loo, if that's the only place that you won't be disturbed. You'll find audio guidance on track 3 of the download. Follow this for the first few days; after that, see if you can do the meditation by yourself without using the track.

Whenever you need clarity of thought – or a creative lift – the Breathing Space is waiting.

90-Second Breathing Space meditation[13]

Step 1: Arriving

Adopt an erect but dignified posture and gently close your eyes. Bring your awareness to whatever is going on for you right now. Ask yourself: What am I experiencing right *now*?

- What *sensations* are here? Briefly scan your body from the toes to the head. If you notice any tension or unpleasant sensations, gently turn towards them. Accept them as best you can. If you begin to tense around the breath, then let go with each out-breath.

- What *feelings* and emotions are here? Can you let these come and go without pushing away those that you don't like, or grabbing hold of those that you do like?

- What *thoughts* do you notice? See if you can let them come and go without identifying with their content. Look 'at' your thoughts, not 'from inside' them. Remember: *thoughts are not facts*.

Step 2: Focusing

Allow your awareness to gather around the sensations the breath makes as it flows into and out of the body. Follow the breath all the way in and all the way out. Use it to anchor your awareness in the present moment. Each time that you notice that your mind has wandered, gently escort your awareness back to the breath.

Step 3: Expanding

Gently broaden and expand your awareness to include the whole body. Imagine your whole body is breathing. If you sense any tension or discomfort, then include this also. Imagine breathing into it with a sense of compassion. You are exploring and befriending it, rather than trying to change it. If the sensations stop tugging for your attention, then return to feeling the whole body breathing.

Now broaden your awareness even more to become aware of any other people who may be around you. Notice any sounds and smells. Gently open your eyes and move your body. As you re-engage with your day, see if you can carry the awareness that you've cultivated with you.

HABIT RELEASER

Over the next week carry out one of the following two Habit Releasers. If you have the time, you might like to do both. You can easily combine the two, as they can follow on logically from each other.

Shop differently

Supermarkets are masters at manipulating our habits. Have you ever wondered why they stock their fresh fruit and vegetables near the entrance to the store? Once you've stocked up on fresh produce (and begun to feel a little more virtuous) you are more likely to buy high-margin processed food further into the shop. Have you noticed that you always turn to the right when you first enter a shop? Virtually everyone does and supermarkets capitalise on this by filling the right side of their stores with their highest-margin products. Have you ever felt annoyed that the products on the shelves seem to be arranged without any obvious sense of order? Or perhaps your favourite items have been moved for no apparent reason? This is to exploit your subconscious instinct to linger a little longer, and to look at a wider range of products, while you try to make sense of the apparent disorder. There are countless similar marketing techniques that are used to persuade you to buy products that you would not normally consider.

One day this week, you should try to break your normal shopping habits by doing one of three things:

1. When you go food shopping make sure that you take an exhaustive list with you. You should not buy anything that's not on the list, no matter how much you want it.

2. Go to a farmers' market or to local independent retailers such as a greengrocer or a bakery. Buy whatever takes your fancy.

3. Shop in a different supermarket – one that you would never normally consider. For example, if you normally go to an 'up-market' retailer, switch to a 'budget' one instead.

The aim of this exercise is to observe your own reactions as you shop – not to buy less (or more), but simply to watch the immense power of your habits. So it's an act of observation, rather than a political or anti-consumerist exercise. The important thing is to move outside your 'comfort zone' and a little into the unknown. And once again, as best you can, try not to judge your thoughts, feelings, emotions and reactions, but simply observe them.

When you first enter the shop or market, make a mental note of the time. Observe your body's reactions when you step over the threshold. Does your body want to slow down or head in any particular direction? How does it feel? Is it a gentle, seductive pull or an irresistible force? Try not to alter your reaction in any way, but simply observe it. What can you see, hear and smell? Can you sense your pupils dilating or shrinking? Does each area of the shop have a different smell? Does your sense of hearing become more or less acute? Can you hear advertising jingles in your mind? Do you feel uplifted and thrilled to be surrounded by such abundance or overwhelmed by it? If you are in a budget shop or a local retailer, do you feel relieved to be surrounded by simplicity or frustrated by it? As you shop, do your arms lift themselves and put the items in your basket or bag automatically, or are you making fully conscious decisions? How do you react when you see the prices? Are you horrified, pleasantly surprised or indifferent? If another shopper brushes against you, how do you react? Look at the other shoppers: do they seem to be fully conscious and aware of what is happening around them? Try not to judge them in any way, but simply observe their behaviour in the way that an anthropologist might study a distant civilisation. When you leave the shop remember to have a look at the time. How long did you spend in the store? Did you spend more (or less) time than you expected?

If you went shopping with a list, did you stick to it? If you didn't, try not to criticise yourself, but make a mental note of how you felt when you ignored the list. If you went to a different store or to a market or individual shops, did you enjoy it less or more? Did you feel more conscious and aware? Did you buy more or less? Did you enjoy the food more or less?

Walk for thirty minutes or more

There is something about the fluid nature of walking that encourages the mind to flow freely and feel at ease with new ideas. Research suggests that 'creative output' can increase by 60 per cent after a short walk.[14] Countless generations of poets, writers, philosophers and artists have known this, and often walked for inspiration. Walking also encourages clarity of mind and purpose, which is why Steve Jobs hiked in the hills above San Francisco with his designers and board members before making important decisions. And he wasn't unique – Aristotle, Einstein, President Obama and even Facebook founder Mark Zuckerberg all walked to clarify their ideas.

For these reasons, this week's second Habit Releaser is to go for a walk for thirty minutes or more. You can walk more or less anywhere. Your neighbourhood is as good as the wild mountains if you walk with the appropriate frame of mind. If you are feeling a little more adventurous, then go somewhere a little wilder such as a nature reserve or the seaside. The important thing is to soak up the surroundings as mindfully as you can, so try to approach the walk with open-minded, playful curiosity. If you are not physically fit, don't worry. The aim is not to push your physical boundaries, but to open up your awareness to new (or perhaps forgotten) states of mind and to notice the effect that walking has on your thought processes.

Before you start walking, spend a few minutes absorbing the scene. What can you see, hear and smell? Does the air have a taste? Focus on the sounds. Soak up the different ones. Can you hear the wind? Or perhaps the notes of different car engines in the distance? Can you hear insects, birdsong or the scampering of small animals such as squirrels? Notice the rise and fall of each individual sound.

Mentally flick between them. How does the pavement, earth or grass feel beneath your feet? As you walk, notice the movement of your muscles and joints. Feel the gentle swaying of your limbs. Can you feel the movement of the breath in your whole body – at the front, the back and the sides? Can you feel how the breath is always changing, just as the sounds do?

If you are walking through the city, look up and pay attention to the buildings. Can you see any wildlife such as nesting birds? Are there any trees or grasses growing out from walls or roofs? What details can you see on the buildings? You might see sculptures, or perhaps dates carved into stonework or even a gargoyle or two. Simply observe with playful curiosity whatever you find.

When you finish your walk, how do you feel mentally and physically? Tired or energised? Achy or pleasantly relaxed? Whatever you feel is what you feel.

CHAPTER SIX

Week Three: Resilience

S hortly after the British mountaineer George Mallory dis-
   appeared while attempting to climb Everest in 1924, a
journalist asked why the team had continued with their assault on
the summit on that fateful day.

'The price of life is death,' replied one of the survivors.

That single sentence sums up the human condition more than
any other. We are here on this earth for a short while, experience
a panoply of bittersweet emotions and then depart. We forget this
at our peril. And yet many of us avoid relating to our most poign-
ant emotions, as much as we can, for as long as we can – usually
until it is too late. While this is often considered normal, especially
among 'high achievers', it carries a high but largely hidden price.
For if we do not allow ourselves to be moved by such emotions as
kindness, compassion, empathy and love, then we cannot fully
embrace life and all of the opportunities it presents. Such emotional aversion closes down the mind, reduces creativity and leaves

behind it a deep-seated sense of fear and caution. It also means that we run the risk of dulling our awareness to all that is wonderful about life, in all of its tingling beauty.

Emotional aversion is driven largely by the 'inner critic'. This voice seeks to protect us from life's difficulties by undermining the emotions that open us up to the risk of pain or disappointment. It rails against the 'risks' of trust, kindness, compassion, empathy and even love. *Life is tough*, it says. *Everyone is in it for themselves. Men are all the same ... Women are all the same ... There's no point doing a good job here ... Anyone who speaks out gets stamped on.* Such harsh cynicism can turn ever further inwards. So the inner critic can end up attacking any signs of kindness, understanding or compassion directed towards yourself: *Why can't I do this? Why is everyone else better than me? Why am I so weak? There's nothing I can do about it ... so don't be stupid ...*

Left to itself, the inner critic will try to fortify you against disappointment and failure by undermining hope for a better future. If you have little hope, then you cannot be disappointed, so the inner critic closes down the parts of the mind dedicated to seeking out new opportunities and ideas. So you can end up in a state akin to low-level depression; a place where you are neither happy nor sad, but exist in a netherworld without hope. If this continues, then you can start to feel burned-out, empty, exhausted – and eventually depressed.

Although the inner critic can seem harsh, cynical and hostile, it is not trying to undermine you. It is, instead, trying to protect you in the only way it knows how: by attacking the thoughts, feelings and emotions that may open you up to the risks of pain and disappointment. This is why it so often rails against the 'positive' emotions of love, kindness, compassion, hope and empathy. It fears that if these emotions do take root, then you will become soft and defenceless in the face of a hostile world. And yet these emotions exist for a reason – and they are of profound importance for creativity and overall success in life.

Over the past decade research has shown that positive emotions not only make people happier, but also more adaptable, creative and healthier. This is because they broaden the mind and open it up to new opportunities. These emotions are regulated by the soothing-and-contentment system that we saw in Chapter Two (see page 23). This, as you may recall, tends to operate when you feel safe and all of your basic needs have been met. It encourages more sophisticated and creative styles of thinking that are able to draw on subtle concepts and ideas, allowing you, in effect, to spot opportunities more easily and then build upon them.

'Negative' emotions stand in stark contrast. Emotions such as fear, anger, bitterness and cynicism narrow the focus of attention. These emotions are governed largely by the 'threat-avoidance' system that we saw in Chapter Two (see page 15), which tends to operate when you feel under pressure. It helps you to make quick decisions, but these can carry a hefty price. Because the brain has only limited processing power, quick decisions can only be made if you rely on habits, reflexes and mental shortcuts. So the 'negative' emotions of fear and anger – and any anxiety, stress and unhappiness that you may be feeling – narrow the mind. They compel you to always look on the bleak side of life. It's the negativity bias and it ensures that you are less able to draw on useful concepts and ideas – and less able to juggle them in your mind to create something new. So overall you become less flexible, adaptable and creative.

In practice, this means that if you feel safe and at peace with yourself, and able to accept all of your faults and foibles, you will become more creative, adaptable and intelligent – and far happier too. In the words of one of the world's leading experts on the role that emotions play in success and overall mental and physical health, Dr Barbara Fredrickson of the University of North Carolina at Chapel Hill: 'When people open their hearts to positive emotions, they seed their own growth in ways that transform them for the better.'[1]

Dr Fredrickson says that cultivating positive emotions helps to build four key resources that progressively enhance success and overall happiness, helping you to meet life's challenges more effectively and to take advantage of its opportunities:

- Firstly, it helps to build *cognitive* resources, such as the ability to mindfully attend to the present moment. This, in turn, enhances concentration, creativity and focus.

- Secondly, it helps to build *psychological* resources, such as the ability to maintain a sense of mastery over life. This can help ward off anxiety, stress, depression and feelings of being trapped or exhausted.

- Thirdly, it builds *social* resources, such as the ability to give and receive emotional support. This helps to build and maintain family ties and friendships.

- Fourthly, it helps build *physical* resources by, for example, boosting the immune system, so that you are healthier and more energised by life.

But cultivating positive emotions is clearly easier said than done. Nobody chooses to be unhappy or stressed any more than they choose to be unsuccessful or devoid of creativity. These distressing states of mind creep up on us over many months and years until they become all consuming. What's needed is a way of actively encouraging positive emotions, rather than simply trying to think – or brainwash – ourselves into feeling happier.

Research has shown that it is possible to do this using a specific type of meditation known as Metta.[2] In a landmark study, Dr Fredrickson and her colleagues at the University of North Carolina found that practising this meditation increased the pleasure and intensity of feelings as diverse as curiosity, amusement, hope, joy, awe and love.[3] These positive emotions then built the four key personal resources necessary for a happy and creative life, namely: *cognitive, psychological, social* and *physical*. This meant that those who practised the meditation found themselves with an increased purpose in life, had more friends, were happier and healthier and were, consequently, more satisfied with their lives. And over time, such feelings lead to enhanced creativity, clarity of thought and cognitive flexibility. It's a virtuous circle too: happiness leads to success – and success leads to greater happiness. And these aren't just welcome outcomes in themselves because research has discovered that such positive moods also directly enhance divergent thinking, the type of thinking which underpins creativity.[4]

Research carried out at other universities has shown that the Metta meditation has many other profound and wide-ranging benefits. For example, it directly quietens the nagging voice of the inner critic.[5] Relentless self-criticism not only hinders creativity but also undermines the other major driving forces behind success, such as courage and resilience. This can be a major problem because if you wish to become truly creative and successful in life, you need the courage to follow your ideas wherever they should lead and the resilience to cope with attacks upon them. Courage and resilience are also vital to help you cope with the inevitable failures. This spirit is essential if you wish to create anything of value. Great art, design, science and engineering are often built on failure. No great books have been written by authors who were satisfied with their work. And no perfect decisions have ever been made, just less imperfect ones. To succeed in any field you need to accept failure as an inevitable part of the creative process. And to do this, great courage and resilience are required.

Once again, it is far easier to say such things than it is to put them into practice. Dealing with the inner critic can be extremely difficult and many of the ways we choose to do so end up being counterproductive. This is largely because the natural reaction to the inner critic is to argue with it; to go on the offensive. But this is precisely the wrong approach. For when you argue with the inner critic, it is like adding yet more fuel to the flames. You are simply giving even more momentum to the mind's Doing mode. The only way out of this vicious cycle is to step aside from the fray and refuse the inner critic's terms of engagement. You need to calm it down – to pacify it – so that it loses impetus and begins to gain a sense of perspective. And countless studies have now confirmed that using the Metta meditation is one of the most effective ways of doing this.

There are many other benefits to practising the Metta meditation. Those who use it tend to have healthier hearts and circulatory systems.[6] Such people also tend to have better chromosomal health or, more specifically, longer telomeres. Telomeres are structures that protect the ends of each chromosome. They shorten with age and are therefore used as indicators of biological age. Several studies have now shown that those who practise Metta meditation have *longer* telomeres, indicating that they are biologically younger than their chronological age would suggest.[7] Metta meditation also enhances emotional and social intelligence.[8] Both are vital skills in an increasingly frantic and complex world. And imaging studies show that this type of meditation increases grey-matter volume in the parts of the brain dedicated to emotional processing[9] – so it helps with emotional stability and ensures that destructive emotions will have less control over your life. These benefits not only accrue, but are also permanent. In practice, this means that over time you will find positive moods arise more easily and feelings of anxiety, stress and depression dissipate more quickly. Nor is it necessary to spend all of your time in a heightened state of reverie to gain these benefits (if such a thing were possible). Research has shown that practising Metta meditation for as little as eight minutes a day can be enough.[10] And it is to this meditation that we will turn in a moment.

Practices for Week Three

- Ten minutes of Breathing meditation (see pages 65–8; track 1 of the download), to be carried out once a day.

- Ten minutes of Resilience meditation – a type of Metta meditation (see pages 19–23; track 4 of the download) – to be carried out once a day.

- 90-Second Breathing Space meditation (see pages 101–2; track 3 of the download), whenever you feel the need.

- A Habit Releaser (see pages 129–33).

BECAUSE IT IS THERE

Week One of the mindfulness programme helped you to train your mind to focus more easily. In the long run, this will help you to gather and integrate new ideas and information, directly enhancing clarity of thought and, ultimately, divergent thinking. You probably found the Breathing meditation intensely frustrating because the mind refused to be still and was easily distracted. This may have become even more frustrating in Week Two. After all, it is easy to accept that the first week of any programme could be difficult, but surely the second should be easier? If it is any consolation, even experienced meditators can have difficulty with this meditation. The mind is designed to think and will rarely remain still. You probably also discovered just how much your mind chatters. Again, this is entirely normal. Chatter is simply the mind's running commentary on the world as it tries to make sense of things and weave it all into a coherent narrative. If you are still frustrated by this meditation, it's worth remembering that the mind's turmoil *is* the meditation. The Breathing meditation is designed to reveal the mind's toings and froings. It is designed to reveal the mind's Doing mode and the gravitational pull of the autopilot, and thereby develop your metacognitive awareness. Without a wandering mind to observe, you cannot learn how the mind works.

Week Two of the programme took these ideas further with the Sounds and Thoughts meditation. This will have begun to reveal the similarities between sounds and thoughts. That is, thoughts (like sounds) arrive seemingly from nowhere and you have virtually no control over their content. Through this you will have begun to learn that 'loud' habitual thoughts – just like intrusive sounds – are the noise that clouds creative insight. Although you may not have noticed it yet, training your mind in this way will have begun to streamline your thought processes. This will help you think more clearly and process information more effectively. It will also have begun to enhance your working memory and to broaden your awareness, so that you can more easily put things into context and juggle information and ideas more effectively. Taken together, these cognitive improvements will have begun to enhance divergent thinking by helping your more subtle and creative ideas to rise above the mind's background noise. This process can take more time than any of us might wish, but the evidence is clear: these benefits will have started to accrue and will continue to build through the rest of the programme.

This week we will take these ideas even further with two meditations. The first is the Breathing meditation. This is the same one that you have practised for the past two weeks. Practising this meditation each day will embed and extend the gains that you have already made.

THE RESILIENCE MEDITATION

The second practice for this week is the Resilience meditation, which is a type of Metta meditation. This enhances creativity in two broad ways. Firstly, it works by directly cultivating positive emotions, which, in turn, lead to greater overall success in life (see Dr Fredrickson's work, page 111). It's a virtuous cycle too, whereby success leads to such positive emotions as happiness, and happiness leads to success.

Secondly, the Resilience meditation will soothe and quieten your inner critic. The inner critic hampers creativity by judging ideas before they are fully formed. Following ideas wherever they should lead is the essence of creativity. Judging or criticising them before they have crystallised tends to fuel the threat-avoidance system. This narrows the mind. It's a vicious cycle whereby the inner critic stimulates this system – and this, in turn, fuels the inner critic. The Resilience meditation helps you to rebalance your mind by stimulating the soothing-and-contentment system. This pacifies the threat-avoidance system and progressively broadens the mind, helping you to access more subtle and sophisticated ways of thinking (both conscious and unconscious) and allowing you to access deeply buried ideas, memories and concepts. In a sense, the place of safety opened up by the soothing-and-contentment system is akin to a giant playroom where anything and every-thing can be explored in a spirit of kindness and curiosity. There is no fear of failure, of ridicule or of loss. It is the arena of possibilities.

The Resilience meditation has five steps. You are asked to bring feelings of warmth, kindness and compassion to a loved one and to dwell on this for a while. You are then asked to transfer these feel-ings first to yourself and then on to an ever-widening circle of other people. Traditionally, people began this meditation by bringing loving kindness to themselves and then transferring these feelings to a loved one. We will start by bringing these feelings to a loved one and then later transferring them to ourselves. We'll do it this way round because many of us find it difficult to bring such loving kindness to ourselves. This is especially true for people who work in the creative industries or other hypercritical, fast-paced organi-sations. These jobs have become so immensely pressured that any form of self-compassion, kindness or empathy is often regarded as a sign of weakness. In these environments, aggression and snap deci-sion making (both of which are fear in disguise) are seen as assets, rather than the liabilities that they truly are. So it's a great irony that organisations which claim to value intelligence, creativity and subtlety of thought often cultivate the very emotions that undermine these qualities.

You might feel that the language in the Resilience meditation seems a little soft and occasionally nebulous. This is deliberate. The words are trying to convey emotion, so they are, of necessity, a little imprecise. So when you carry out this meditation, try to engage with the spirit of the practice, rather than focusing on the exact meaning of the words. If you should find yourself pulling away from the softness of the language, it will pay to remember that this is the reaction of your inner critic – the part of you that is trying its hardest to toughen you up, so that you can be strong enough to survive in a seemingly harsh world. This reaction is entirely understandable. Your inner critic is doing its best to protect you by erecting barriers to keep out any signs of weakness. So, if this should happen, gently acknowledge the help that this part of you is trying to give by smiling warmly to yourself. Focus on the thoughts and feelings that are welling up inside you, and then watch as they dissipate. Then you can re-engage with the underlying warmth and kindness of the meditation. It is these feelings of warmth and kindness that are central to the meditation, and they are far more important than the actual words that you will be asked to say to yourself; try to remember this as you carry it out.

In a sense, this meditation is quite different from the other ones in the programme. All of the others ask you to observe your mind and the world around you without actually trying to change anything. They ask you to accept what you find with as much kindness and curiosity as you can muster. The Resilience meditation is different in that it asks you to actively engage and to visualise the changes that you wish to see in yourself. Such visualisation can be extremely powerful, not just on a psychological level but on a physical one too. Research has shown, for example, that athletes who have been asked to visualise increases in speed and strength actually become faster and stronger, and this is also reflected in increased muscle mass.[11]

To summarise, this week you are working on the mind in two different ways. The Breathing meditation asks you to focus on the breath and thereby enhance mental clarity; it does this by helping you to make peace with your most turbulent thoughts. The Resilience meditation asks you to bring a sense of warmth, kindness and compassion to yourself and to others; this dampens the inner critic and cultivates positive emotions, which, in turn, stimulate a different and more open style of thinking.

This week's Habit Releasers work in a similar vein (you are once again asked to choose between one of two). They are designed to help you rebalance your daily life to help you fully engage with the warm feelings of kindness, compassion and empathy. These will strengthen the soothing-and-contentment system, so that you can develop a more open, inquisitive, friendly and compassionate approach to life.

Practicalities

It is best to carry out both of this week's meditations at different times of the day on six days out of the next seven. It is entirely up to you when you do them, although most people tend to practise the Breathing meditation in the morning and the Resilience meditation in the evening. Both are best carried out in warm and quiet surroundings, so remember to arrange not to be disturbed.

It's a good idea to refresh your mind about the practicalities of meditation before you start (see pages 46–50), and read the meditation guidance below to familiarise yourself with the techniques. It is best if you listen to the audio track for the Resilience meditation while you actually carry it out. After a few days of practice, you might like to extend this meditation by sitting quietly for a while after the track has finished. Many people do this quite naturally. Another option is to do an additional Breathing meditation immediately prior to the Resilience one. If you do this, make sure that the combined meditation is just one of your daily sessions. This increases the effectiveness of the whole programme, but it is up to you whether you do it or not.

This week, the Breathing meditation is slightly different in that you are urged to carry it out without the guidance of the audio track. Learning to meditate without guidance is an important skill and most people begin after about two or three weeks of practice.

Resilience meditation

Track 4

Sit upright in a straight-backed chair. Allow your spine to adopt its natural shape in a relaxed but dignified posture about an inch from the back of the chair. Let your eyes close gently.

Begin by tuning into the world around you. It might be noisy outside. You might hear cars, wind, rain, air-conditioning, birds or human voices. Whatever is here, focus your awareness on these sounds for a few moments. Remain receptive to them, rather than being drawn into them. Try not to change anything. Simply listen to this 'soundscape' for a few moments.

Gently gather up your awareness and bring it to the breath. Follow the breath in and out for a few moments. If your mind should wander, gently note where it went and escort it back to the breath. Allow your body to be soft; your mind to be soft.

When you are ready, bring to mind a loved one, a child perhaps, or even a cherished pet – someone you love unconditionally. Bring to mind an image of them. Or perhaps a sense of them. When you have a sense of your love for them, gently repeat these phrases in your mind:

May they be safe and free from suffering.
May they feel happy and healthy.
May they live with ease.
Happy, safe, fulfilled.

Allow the time for these phrases to settle. Imagine them to be pebbles that are dropped, one by one, down a deep well. You are listening for any echoes that arise. These echoes might be thoughts, feelings, sensations or urges. Be curious about them. There is no need to judge. Take this time to feel warmth and kindness for them.

Once you have a sense of your love for them, gently expand it to include yourself. Bring this sense of warmth and loving kindness to yourself. Imagine it soaking into your skin, into your body, into your bones ... bringing peace in its wake. Gently repeat the following phrases in your mind:

May I be safe and free from suffering.
May I feel happy and healthy.

May I live with ease.
Happy, safe, fulfilled.

Let yourself bask in this loving kindness, breathing it in, and then breathing it out. Allow yourself to feel love and acceptance of yourself. Allow yourself to be exactly as you are.

When you are ready, bring to mind another person, someone who you don't know very well but see from time to time. Someone neutral. They also have a life full of hopes and fears, just like you. When you have a clear sense of them, gently expand your warmth and kindness towards them, to greet them. Imagine them bathed in the light of your kindness. Gently repeat the phrases:

May they be safe and free from suffering.
May they feel happy and healthy.
May they live with ease.
Happy, safe, fulfilled.

Take your time between the phrases. Allow the words to settle. Feel the warmth. Be curious about any thoughts, feelings or sensations that arise.

When you are ready, bring to mind someone who you are having difficulties with at the moment. It might be a colleague, family member, a neighbour or perhaps someone you met recently at work, in the street or while travelling. It needn't be the most difficult person in your life, just someone who you are having trouble with. As best you can, try to bring a little warmth or acceptance to them as you repeat the phrases to yourself:

May they be safe and free from suffering.
May they feel happy and healthy.
May they live with ease.
Happy, safe, fulfilled.

Be curious about any thoughts, feelings or sensations that arise. As best you can, try to bring a sense of acceptance and kindness to these feelings – and then to the other person. You do not have to forgive them. Simply accept the situation as it is, for now.

When you are ready, imagine your warmth and kindness spreading ever farther outwards. Feel or imagine how it extends in every direction, in front and behind, to the left and to the right, above and below. Imagine its warmth flowing outwards … enveloping your home, your neighbourhood, your town or city … the whole world … and all of the living creatures that also call it home. They also wish to be safe, happy, fulfilled … They also want to live a happy and bountiful life. Gently repeat the phrases to yourself:

May all of us be safe and free from suffering.
May all of us feel happy and healthy.
May we all live with ease.
Happy, safe, fulfilled.

Allow yourself as much time as you wish to be with the breath. As you sit here, know that these feelings are always open to you. They are only ever a few moments away. A single breath away.

When you are ready, bring this meditation to a close. What can you hear? What can you smell? What can you feel on your skin? Gently open your eyes and soak up whatever is in your line of sight. Gradually, gently, begin to move, giving yourself enough time to make a smooth transition from the meditation to whatever you're doing next.

'No right or wrong way to feel'

How do you feel when you do this meditation? Although there is no right or wrong way to feel, some people have quite powerful reactions.

Nick said he felt 'a bit daft' doing it: 'It felt a bit hippyish and "religious" in the sense that we're all supposed to love each other (especially our enemies) and then everything will be OK ... Except everything isn't OK. I've been having a very stressful time at work. The department has been in turmoil for months with one reorganisation following another. My boss is a stress monster and everyone around me is losing the plot. All I want is enough peace and quiet to get on with my job, and this meditation asks me to love everyone. Who exactly was I supposed to bring loving kindness to? My boss? My bad-tempered colleagues? Difficult customers? Lots of people in my life right now are just plain difficult and I spend a lot of time trying not to get angry about them. The only release is my painting, but even that has become stilted and angry.'

Ginnie faced similar difficulties. She was also under a lot of pressure at work and could not see the point of bringing warmth and kindness to strangers. And she had extreme difficulty bringing it to her sister, with whom she'd always had a very fraught relationship. 'I got to the bit in the meditation where I was asked to bring loving kindness to "someone who you are having difficulties with at the moment". I tried focusing on my sister, but my mind instantly veered away. So I tried again and I just felt annoyed, and then my mind was flooded with angry memories. I even began to run through arguments we'd had as teenagers. I could not accept that being kind and loving to my sister – or anyone else that I found difficult – was going to help me with my life and work.'

These reactions are entirely normal. After all, if you are under a lot of pressure, it *is* hard to bring a sense of warmth to the most difficult people in your life. Should you face this common problem, then try bringing someone slightly less contentious to mind. Try someone who you find slightly annoying, difficult or awkward, rather than someone you actively dislike or even hate. The aim of this meditation is to cultivate kindness, not to become a saint.

If you still struggle with this aspect of the meditation, it's also worth remembering that you are not expected to feel love for *everyone* all of the time. The idea behind the meditation is to gently rebalance your mind away from such negative emotions as fear and anger; if you can't manage love, then warmth or kindness will do. The underlying theme of this meditation is to constantly expand your field of warmth and kindness outwards as a form of exercise for your emotional 'muscles'. This is not always easy, but then nobody tries to get fit at the gym by only ever tackling the easiest exercises. And the same is true with this meditation. It is inherently calming because it stimulates the soothing-and-contentment system. And, over time, these feelings will grow so that you become less reactive and significantly happier. You will become quicker to laugh and slower to anger. It will give you the courage to experiment, to play with ideas and to risk failure.

This meditation works on another level too: it enhances mental flexibility by teaching you how to effortlessly shift perspective. A good way of picturing this is to look at the contrast between the Resilience and Breathing meditations. The Resilience meditation broadens your mental perspective, whereas the Breathing meditation encourages a more precisely focused form of concentration. Repeatedly moving between these two perspectives teaches you how to shift the 'lens' of your awareness in and out. See it as a zoom lens that can focus on tiny details and then open up to capture a wide panorama. This ability to shift between different perspectives – different flavours of awareness – is an important aspect of creativity.

'I just wanted a break from myself'

As difficult as it can be to bring kindness to someone that you do not like, it can be even tougher to bring it to yourself. This is especially true if you've spent many years working hard and goading yourself on to ever greater achievements. These patterns can wear very deep tracks in the mind.

'All of the way through this meditation my mind kept on attacking me,' said Becca. 'There was a constant stream of bitterness and doubt – and a craving for things to be different. My mind kept saying stuff like, *This is just stupid. How can bringing warmth and kindness to yourself possibly work?* I found it easier to bring genuine love to others – especially to the whole world – than to myself. I could not bring it to myself, no matter how hard I tried. It was just not working. After a lot of consideration, I realised that it was my approach to my job that was the problem. I work for an environmental NGO, so I'm used to looking at the big picture and putting the environment and wider society first. I work hard (no time for sleep on a dying planet, as they say) and rely on my wits to get things done. This means that I'm constantly exhausted and get to see my own flaws with crystal clarity. I suppose I seek perfection in myself, but then again, I do know that I can make a positive difference to the world. I took up mindfulness to help me work more effectively and to produce creative solutions to environmental and social problems. I don't particularly want to love myself. I just want to escape the part of myself that's dragging me down.'

If your inner critic attacks you in this way, then gently smile inwardly to yourself and say, 'Angry thoughts, angry thoughts', 'Fearful thoughts, fearful thoughts' or whatever feels most appropriate. You can then return the focus of your awareness to the breath for a few moments before continuing with the meditation where you left off.

If you still find it difficult to bring warm feelings to yourself, then you might try bringing a measure of strategic acceptance to the meditation. This is simply the acceptance of the situation as it is – for now. In practice, this means ceasing to struggle against your thoughts, feelings and emotions. Simply accept them for what they are: patterns of thoughts and feelings in your mind. Try to remember that *you are not your thoughts*. As best you can, watch them play out in your mind. And when their turmoil begins to subside, try bringing a little warmth, kindness and compassion to them. Sometimes just accepting that cultivating kindness is difficult can remove most of the doubts and fears that are holding you back. Paradoxically, accepting that something is difficult can make it far easier.

When the meditation is over, if the inner critic should still attack you for trying to bring kindness to yourself, you might like to remind yourself of what science has shown: the Resilience meditation works. It does enhance creativity and clarity of thought. It does reduce anxiety, stress and depression, while enhancing overall mental and physical health. And, over time, these will help you to build the personal resources necessary for a happy and successful life. In short, you will become more resilient to life's ups and downs.

'It worked for me'

Lois found that bringing strategic acceptance to her inner critic helped her enormously. Her hobby is writing fiction, and learning to accept (and to learn from) failure is crucial to success.

'I had a particularly well-developed inner critic,' said Lois. 'It was so well developed that it often crippled my writing. So the Resilience meditation proved a godsend to me. Spending a little time each day cultivating kindness towards myself and my work has transformed my writing. Looking back, it was quite obvious where I was going wrong and how the meditations, particularly the Resilience meditation, worked. I was sorely lacking in self-esteem. It wasn't obvious to other people, but it became increasingly obvious to me. This seeped through to my writing, so that I found it very difficult to write. I would type out a few sentences, decide that they were rubbish and then delete them. This would go on for hour after hour and day after day. It became so bad that I simply felt like a complete and utter failure all day long.

'The Resilience meditation gave me the courage to start writing, even though I felt like a failure and had no idea where my storylines would lead. There's a saying: "Writers would sooner pick the hairs out of the plughole at the bottom of the shower than write." That was certainly the case for me! So simply being able to start was a great help. It also helped me make some kind of peace with my inner critic. It helped me to continue writing, even though it was attacking me all of the time. Before I started the programme it never occurred to me that writers, indeed anyone in the creative industries, needed courage to succeed. I assumed that courage was only needed by those facing physical danger, but that's just not the case. If you face any situation that has the power to threaten your self-esteem, then you need courage if you wish to succeed.

'Over time it has become clear the ways that mindfulness has helped my writing. It's helped me to become aware of the ways that the autopilot can distract me, and given me the ability to move past it into a creative zone. It's also helped me to notice those moments of inspiration amid the whirlwind of a stressful job. It's helped me question my assumptions and to follow imaginative ideas to see how they develop. Mindfulness has heightened my awareness of negative thoughts as they arise and their impact on me too. I've now learned to turn them around by simply acknowledging them as random, almost unreal, and this has improved my confidence in my writing and overall creative abilities.

'I've also learned to accept my frustration and to move through it, or rather to take notice of what that frustration is telling me, instead of fighting it. I've often found that frustration is trying to tell me that my mind is working on the problem in the background. It's kind of like my mind is waving a flag at me. It's almost like an energy that progressively builds. I can feel the frustration build and build almost until I'm exhausted and then, after a day or two, the energy is released and I can write brilliantly. When it happens it's almost like someone else is writing for me. Everything comes out fully formed. It's almost like I'm not there – like I'm some kind of spectator. The Resilience meditation has given me the courage to *know* that this will eventually happen. To be patient. To allow ideas to develop deep inside my mind and then to burst outwards fully formed when they're good and ready.'

HABIT RELEASER

Over Week Three carry out one of the following two Habit Releasers. If you have the time, you might like to do both.

Go to the seaside (or the mountains)

A trip to the seaside can reinvigorate the soul like nothing else. The sense of space and fresh air opens the mind to new horizons. A few hours of ambling along a seafront or a wild and windswept beach puts everything in perspective. Even your most pressing worries simply dissolve when you spend a little time gazing at the horizon.

It's important to mentally set aside the time now for this Habit Releaser, otherwise it might get squeezed out by seemingly more important things or perhaps a change in the weather will be used as an excuse. It's important to go regardless of the weather. A walk along the seashore in a rainstorm can be an amazing experience. It will make you feel truly alive!

Try and go to your nearest beach or seaside town, prefer-ably one you've never been to before, rather than one of the better-known resorts. If you're a regular visitor to your nearest seaside town, try visiting one further afield. You'll probably get far more out of a visit to a down-at-heel town or unglamorous beach than a major attraction. Try to remember that this Habit Releaser, like the whole of this week's programme, is designed to reconnect you with your empathic and kindly heart, so take your time and allow yourself to enjoy the day. See it as a licence to be five years old again. (You can even eat candy floss if you want!)

Just before you arrive, whether by train or car, think about how you feel? Is there a sense of anticipation? Where is it localised? In the stomach, throat or hands? When you do arrive, how does the air feel? Warm, cool or bitterly cold? What does it smell like? See if you can sense all of the different aromas, from the saltiness of the sea to the vinegaryness of chips and mushy peas. Walk aimlessly towards the sea. If something catches your eye, feel free to move closer, and spend as much time as you want looking at it. If you are in a town or village, have a look at the buildings. Again, just explore – there are no rules on this day. The same spirit applies if you visit a wilder beach with no buildings near by at all. Do whatever takes your fancy.

Look out to sea and focus on the horizon. What can you see? Yachts, ships or perhaps oil rigs and wind turbines? And the beach – is it wet or dry, sandy or muddy? And the seafront or seashore. Allow all of your senses to explore whatever is near by.

What will you have to eat and drink? Treat yourself to whatever you feel like. This is a day for enjoying all that the material world has to offer. Mindfulness is not against eating, drinking and being merry. It is not austere and unforgiving. It is about being alive and connected to whatever you are doing – so enjoy everything that the seaside has to offer. Serendipity thrives when your heart is at ease and playful.

Note: if you can't make it to the coast, you can adapt this Habit Releaser to suit a visit to a lake or the mountains.

Put others before yourself

Harsh, judgmental and critical thoughts towards others ensure that you are even more critical of yourself.[12] In turn, this sows the seeds of anxiety, stress and depression. This seems like a paradox – after all, we are normally wary and critical of others as a form of self-protection. Surely it's better to be suspicious, rather than take the risk of being used and abused? While this attitude can seem logical, it means you can fall into a pit dug by the mind's negativity bias (see pages 20–5). This encourages you to always look on the bleak side of life and be guarded around others. Such caution carries a big and largely hidden price because it undercuts creativity by stimulating the mind's avoidance systems. But not only that. This attitude also ignores the fact that we are social creatures with an inbuilt desire to help others. Virtually all social interactions are neutral, altruistic or symbiotic. Truly parasitic behaviour is very rare. Nevertheless, suspending judgmentalism can be difficult ... but one of the best ways is to be consciously altruistic. So, one of this week's Habit Releasers is to spend a day putting others before yourself. This can be difficult but here are some pointers:

Why not try carrying out a good-natured deed for someone else? If you are feeling especially confident, you could be kind to someone you normally find difficult or even dislike. Remember that the joy is in the giving, rather than in the gratitude you'll receive in return. You needn't make an extravagant gesture. Even such small things as holding open doors for strangers or buying friends or colleagues a drink count.

Perhaps there is one small thing that you can do for someone else that will improve their day? For example, you might like to help friends or neighbours tidy their house or garden. There are probably many community groups in your area that are desperate for volunteers. Don't feel that you need to offer to help for a whole day (or see it as a long-term, ongoing commitment); they are used to people helping out for only an hour or two. Searching the internet for groups in your area will probably throw up many possibilities. When you actually do the voluntary work, try not to judge others. Accept their differences and the various reasons they have for helping others. You never know, they might be there for entirely altruistic reasons, for companionship or they could even be ex-criminals wishing to make amends. It can be impossible to accurately judge others' intentions, so practise not trying for a day.

At work, if you know that a colleague is hard pressed on a particular job, you might like to leave a little treat on their desk first thing in the morning: a bunch of flowers or a small bar of chocolate could transform their day. If you are feeling especially altruistic, you might like to do it in secret and not claim the credit. Or you might like to help them tidy their desk or make the tea or coffee more frequently than fairness dictates. And while you are doing all this, keep an eye out for similarly kind and compassionate behaviour in others. You might be surprised by how often it occurs.

At home, you could do something that you know your partner hates doing. Or perhaps cook them their favourite food or buy them their favourite wine, beer or cocktail.

We often hold back from helping others out of shyness or from fear of appearing foolish or even weak. Likewise, should you feel the temptation to judge others, perhaps because they are not showing the gratitude you think you deserve, then observe these thoughts, feelings and emotions. Embrace them. What goes around comes around.

CHAPTER SEVEN

Week Four: Insight

I n the hills of southern India, the children have an ingenious way of catching monkeys. They use a trap made from a hollowed-out coconut that's chained to a stake in the ground. Inside the coconut they place some delicious peanuts that can be grabbed through a small hole – a hole that a monkey's empty hand can fit through, but a monkey's fist stuffed with peanuts cannot. So when a hungry monkey grabs the peanuts, it becomes trapped. But not by anything physical. It is trapped by an idea that has served it well for many years: *When you see peanuts, grab them and don't let go!*

Whenever you struggle with a seemingly intractable problem, it is tempting to continue trying to solve it using the full force of the mind, to worrit at it a little bit longer, to try to wriggle your peanut-stuffed fist out of the trap one last time ... As with the monkey, it's an approach that has undoubtedly served you well for many years, so it's not surprising that you would want to continue along the same path. But what if this was precisely the wrong approach? What if the best way of dealing with a complex and nuanced problem was to simply pause for a while, to allow your perspective to broaden, and then to see how things pan out? For many people, this apparently passive approach smacks of heresy, but often as not, it's the best course of action. This is because focusing too intensely on a problem can narrow the mind, close down options and shut the doors to serendipity. It can drive you around in ever-decreasing circles and cripple the creativity that you so desperately need to actually solve the problem. This happens because the mind tends to use its Doing mode to solve complex problems. This, as you will recall, is the mind's rational and logical approach to solving problems (see pages 35–9). It often works brilliantly and the process happens so fast and seamlessly that we rarely see the underlying process. And we only become aware of its limitations when we are stumped by a problem and begin to chase our own tails in an endless, fruitless loop.

By and large, the mind's Doing mode is extremely effective at solving discrete problems where you have detailed knowledge and it is possible to find a logical solution without the need for a creative leap. But it tends to stall when confronted with an insight problem. This is the class of problem where you have incomplete information, the solutions are neither straightforward nor obviously logical, and where finesse, flair, instinct and imaginative leaps are required. Unfortunately, these are precisely the problems that we increasingly face in our fast-paced and frantic world.

Focusing on a problem using the mind's Doing mode is an example of *convergent* thinking and is the opposite of the *divergent* thinking style that propels creativity. This is not to say that there is anything inherently wrong with convergent thinking. On the contrary, the ability to focus intensely on a problem and to logically plough through possible solutions is one of humanity's greatest assets, but it does have downsides – particularly if you are routinely faced with problems that are superficially similar, but quite different beneath the surface. If this happens, then experience can blind the mind to new approaches. Cast your mind back to Chapter Five and the story of the surgeon (see page 79), which required a flash of inspiration – an 'Aha!' moment – to solve. Almost everywhere you look you will find similar insight problems that bamboozle intelligent people who have become blinded by experience. Clearly, then, to effectively solve an *insight* problem a different approach is required. You need a way of broadening and softening your perspective so that the connections between existing ideas can be loosened, allowing new ones to be made. Once again, this is easier said than done. After all, 'The difficulty lies not in the new ideas,' as John Maynard Keynes said, 'but in escaping from the old ones.'

Throughout history, great thinkers have developed ways of broadening their own mental horizons to help them escape from their old habitual thought patterns. Archimedes would take a long bath. Isaac Newton sat under a tree. Wordsworth would go for long, rambling walks. Churchill preferred to take an afternoon nap. Although all of these approaches can be effective, they are short-term solutions that only temporarily change the underlying approach to problem solving. They also rely on changing your external circumstances, which isn't always easy or practical. What's needed is an approach that allows you to fundamentally shift your perspective whenever required. And this, as we saw in Week Two, is best done using an open-monitoring meditation.

Open-monitoring meditations work on many levels simultaneously:

- Firstly, they cultivate the mind's Being mode. As you will recall, the brain switches into this mental 'gear' when you experience the world directly through your senses, without thoughts acting as an intermediary or distorting lens. So instead of thinking *about* the world, you begin to *experience* it directly. This produces a state of pure awareness – of mindfulness – that frees you from your habitual thoughts, feelings, emotions and preconceptions. This radically different perspective directly enhances divergent thinking.

- Secondly, they create great clarity of mind and purpose, so that you can begin to see new ideas as they arise and then to act upon them.

- Thirdly, they enhance cognitive flexibility and working memory. This tends to weaken the hold that habitual thoughts, feelings and emotions have over you.

- Fourthly, they help your deep subconscious to more effectively gather and process information, reformulate problems and to produce new and creative ideas and solutions.

- Fifthly, they dissolve any anxiety, stress or unhappiness that you may be feeling. Although this is obviously a happy outcome in itself, it also stimulates the soothing-and-contentment system which, in turn, rebalances the body's emotional regulation systems. This, ultimately, broadens the mental horizons necessary for creativity to flourish.

- And finally, these meditations promote happiness, which directly enhances creative thought.

Week Two of the programme and the Sounds and Thoughts meditation gave you a first taste of open monitoring. This week we will go significantly further with the Insight meditation.

Practices for Week Four

- Ten minutes of Breathing meditation (see page 65–8; track 1 of the download), to be carried out once a day.

- Ten minutes of Insight meditation (see page 146–9; track 5 of the download), to be carried out once a day. If you prefer, you can use the twenty-minute version of Insight meditation (track 6 of the download).

- 90-Second Breathing Space meditation (see pages 101–2; track 3 of the download), to be carried out as necessary.

- A Habit Releaser (see pages 155–8).

INSIGHT MEDITATION

To be truly creative, you need to master three skills. Firstly, you need an open and disciplined mind that can gather and then integrate new ideas and information. The Breathing meditation promotes such open-minded discipline. Secondly, you need to actually notice new ideas as they emerge from the noisy background of your mind. The

Sounds and Thoughts meditation helped you to begin cultivating this skill. Thirdly, you need the courage to follow your ideas wherever they should lead and the resilience to cope with the inevitable setbacks and criticism. The Resilience meditation helped you to begin enhancing these qualities.

This week we will take these ideas further with the Insight meditation, which welds together the three key elements of the whole mindfulness programme into one powerful practice. It is an open-monitoring meditation that has been used for many centuries to gain insight into the workings of the human mind and to prepare the mental stage ready to think deeply about great philosophical questions. More recently, it has been proven to significantly enhance divergent thinking – the state of mind which, as we know, lies behind 'Aha!' moments and creative leaps.[1] Divergent thinking is the most mysterious state of mind because it summons up ideas, seemingly from nowhere – often out of the blue and frequently without bidding. It's an approach that allows us to spontaneously 'see' the solution to a problem, to conjure up new ideas, and to create a work of art or design with true insight.

The Insight meditation unfolds in two stages: it asks you to focus on the breath for a few minutes to stabilise the mind; then it asks you to sit and wait patiently for a thought, feeling or emotion to emerge from the background hubbub of your mind. After a while, you will realise that you've been swept along by the mind's running commentary on the world. Once you have become aware of this, you should then briefly refocus your mind on the breath, before waiting patiently for another thought, feeling or emotion to arise.

The Insight meditation is similar to the other practices in the programme in that it helps you to become increasingly aware of your thoughts and also of your mind's background chatter. It is similar, too, in that it also encourages you to bring warmth and compassion to your inevitable 'failings'. It does, however, differ in one crucial respect: the *absence* of thoughts, feelings and emotions becomes the central *subject* of your meditation. This allows you to see the moment that a thought bubbles up from your subconscious mind and then begins gathering momentum, ultimately, leading to a whole cascade of other thoughts and emotions. So, focusing on this absence helps you to become progressively more conscious of how your mind actually works. Such an insight isn't just profound in a philosophical sense – it also smooths the path that leads directly from subconscious sources of inspiration towards the conscious mind. It strips away many of the layers of mediation – in effect, distorting lenses – that lie between you and the source of your ideas. Such mediation is often governed by the mind's Doing mode and, of course, is greatly influenced by the autopilot.

Waiting patiently for a thought or emotion to arise can be an unusual experience and, occasionally, a frustrating one. Our heads are normally so full of thoughts that a period of quiet can be an eerie experience. Rest assured, however – it won't last long. Our minds are not wired to wait. The waiting may feel like you are looking at a dark pool. Or it may feel like a void. There might be a sense of unformed thoughts bubbling away in the background of your mind, tantalisingly beyond reach. You may be filled with warm pleasure; a smile may spontaneously appear; you may lose track of time, so that it appears to momentarily pause. You might be filled with expectation, suspense or frustration. Whatever this waiting feels like, sooner or later (usually sooner), a thought or emotion *will* arise. It might be a fully formed concept or, more likely, a seductive 'thoughtlet' that gradually sneaks up on you before crystallising and triggering a whole chain of other thoughts. These can be so powerful and enticing that they sweep you along and ensure that you lose track of where they came from.

One of the great mysteries of science is what gives rise to thoughts and to consciousness itself. Neither you nor I are likely to solve that riddle ... you might, however, begin to notice when thoughts first appear in your mind. And when a thought does appear, it arrives, in effect, in a wide-open mental space created by the Insight meditation that saps it of momentum. An analogy might help. Have you noticed the way people slow down and fall silent when they walk through a door into a wide-open space? A broad expansive awareness has the same effect on thoughts. In this way, the Insight meditation reduces the background noise of your thoughts, so that you can become more aware of the quieter ones. And these quiet thoughts can often be a great source of inspiration. The philosophers of ancient Greece and more modern figures like Steve Jobs have all credited this quiet voice with being the source of their inspiration. If nothing else, tapping into these quieter thoughts can give you a more subtle, insightful approach to life and work. And such changes of tack are often all that is needed to spark a chain of ideas that ultimately leads to a breakthrough, a thought-provoking work of art, or an inspired decision.

Practicalities

This week there are two main meditations to carry out: the Breathing and the Insight meditation. Each should be performed once a day. Although it's up to you when you do them, most people prefer to do the Insight meditation in the morning and the

Breathing one later in the day. There are two Insight meditations for you to download. The first is ten minutes long. The second is twenty. The only difference between the two is the length of the periods of silence between the spoken instructions. So they are identical, apart from the length of the track. You might like to use the ten-minute version for the first three or four days and then switch to the twenty-minute one (track 6) for the remaining days. If you find this meditation particularly difficult, feel free to continue using the ten-minute version throughout. Although in the long run you will gain more benefit from the longer version, it is optional and you should only use it if you feel you have the mental stamina to do it. Meditation tends to be 'dose dependent': that is, the more that you do, the greater the benefit (within reason). As with last week, you should aim to carry out the Breathing meditation without listening to the audio track. Meditating without guidance is an important skill as it allows you to adapt the practice to suit your location and the time available. You should also use the 90-Second Breathing Space meditation whenever you feel the need.

Insight

When you first begin the Insight meditation, cultivating the correct type of awareness can seem a little daunting. There is no need to worry. If you follow the guidelines, it will tend to arise quite naturally. It may take a while, but it will arise. As with all other mindfulness meditations, worrying about whether you are doing it 'right' is the best way of undermining the practice. You cannot fail at meditation – and this is true more than ever for the Insight meditation. There are, however, some recommendations for how to gain the most from this particular meditation:

- Try to remember that the aim of this meditation is not to clear the mind of thoughts. Nor is it to encourage them to appear in your mind. It is simply to train your mind to become aware of the moment that thoughts first appear. In this sense, it's a refinement of both the Breathing and the Sounds and Thoughts meditations. Such a neutral stance allows your mind to become progressively clearer – more insightful – so that your conscious thoughts no longer act as an intermediary between you and your ideas. Over time, this will help you to become more receptive to the new ideas bubbling up from your subconscious mind. This is the driving force behind divergent thinking.

- The essence of this Insight meditation lies in those moments when you are waiting for a thought, feeling or emotion to arise. In the context of this meditation, there are two types of waiting. The first involves a sense of expectation – almost as if you are willing thoughts to appear in your mind. If you can, try to avoid becoming too expectant. Simply wait as patiently as you can. A thought, feeling or emotion will certainly arise – often within moments of the mind first becoming clear. Waiting 'too hard' may cloud the moment – or it might itself trigger a cascade of thoughts. If this should happen, then mentally take a step back while smiling gently to yourself. The second type of waiting involves warm-hearted patience. If possible, try to imbue this patience with a sense of kindness and curiosity. Mindfulness teachers use the word 'equanimous' to describe this state of mind. When a thought, feeling or emotion does arise, gently acknowledge it, then briefly focus on the breath before returning to waiting patiently.

- As best you can, try to imbue your meditation with warmth and kindness. This is especially true when your mind has just wandered for the umpteenth time. Rather than snapping it back to attention, try instead to shepherd it back to the breath, while smiling inwardly to yourself. This will help to embed the benefits of the practice by reinforcing the soothing-and-contentment system. In this sense, it is similar to the Resilience meditation.

- If you feel an emotion – or an urge or impulse to do something – see if you can sense where it is located in the body. If you can find it, gently breathe into that part of the body with a sense of warmth and kindness for a few moments. Be curious about what you find. For example, you might feel fear or excitement located in the stomach, or perhaps an incredible urge to move might be found in your hands or legs. Once again, spend a few moments exploring these sensations and driving forces. Be curious. There is no rush. Once the feelings have subsided, move the focus of your awareness back to the breath for a few moments, and then begin to wait patiently once again.

- As you progress through the meditation, and your mind begins to feel increasingly settled, see if you can broaden your awareness so that your mind feels literally 'wider' and more 'open'. Some people find that imagining their mind becoming progressively 'bigger' and more expansive helps. Another way of looking at this is to imagine that you are wearing old-fashioned blinkers that are steadily widened before finally being removed. It's as if you become gradually more settled and open to everything. Try to gain a sense of the whole world that surrounds you. Once again, as much as you feel able, avoid trying too hard. This is quite an advanced technique that even accomplished meditators can have difficulties with.

- And finally, try to remember that this meditation should not be used to actively solve a problem. If you should try to meditate on a problem, then you will run the risk of kick-starting the mind's Doing mode, rather than its Being mode. This will undermine the effectiveness of the meditation. Over time, this meditation will help you solve problems and enhance your creativity, but if you actively aim to do this, then you will subconsciously begin to narrow your horizons and thereby undermine many of its benefits. This may seem like an annoying paradox, and in some ways it is, but the aim here is to till the soil that will allow your ideas to germinate and grow. This cannot be done if you are constantly digging away and forcing the ideas to take root. You will find, however, that shortly after your meditation session ends, new ideas will begin to spontaneously appear in your mind with increasing frequency.

Insight meditation   Track 5 & Track 6

1. Adopt your usual meditation posture on a straight-backed chair. Place your hands in your lap and allow your shoulders and neck to relax. Begin by gently closing your eyes and tuning into the world around you. It might be noisy outside. You might hear cars, wind, rain, air-conditioning, birdsong or human voices. Whatever is there, pay attention to the sounds for a few moments.

2. Gather up your awareness and move it down to both feet simultaneously for a few moments. What do you feel there? Tune into the actual sensations. There's no need to label what you find or describe it in any way. There is no 'correct' way to feel. Do your feet feel warm or cold? Tired or achy? The sensations may be intense or there might be none at all. It doesn't matter. What matters is that you are aware. Move your attention on to the ankles ... the lower legs ... the knees ... the thighs ... and on to the right hip. Pause for a few moments to take in the sensations from both hips.

3. Move your awareness to both hands at the same time. What do you feel? Tune into the actual sensations without feeling that you need to describe or name them in any way. And your arms? What do they feel like? And your shoulders ... neck ... head ... face ... lips ... nose.

4. As gently as you can, start paying attention to the movement of your breath and the effect it has on your body. Can you feel your chest and stomach swelling on the in-breath and subsiding on the out-breath? Can you feel your back or shoulders stretching and broadening on each in-breath and subsiding on each out-breath? Try not to alter or force the breath in any way, but rest your awareness within its natural movements. Focus your awareness on wherever the sensations of breathing are the strongest. As best you can, focus your awareness on these sensations for a couple of minutes.

5. From time to time your mind will wander. This is entirely normal. Each time it happens, gently acknowledge where it went by saying, 'Thinking, thinking', 'Planning, planning'

or whatever feels most appropriate. After you've acknowledged your mind's wanderings, bring your awareness back to wherever the sensations of breathing are the strongest.

6. After a couple of minutes of focusing on the breath, allow your mind to wait patiently for a thought, feeling or emotion to rise to the surface.

   Thoughts and emotions – and the gaps in between them – are now to become the focus of your meditation.

7. When you become aware of your thoughts, gently acknowledge them. Simply observe them in your mind's eye. Try not to argue with them or engage with them in any way. Remember that *you are not your thoughts*. Notice how they rise and fall in intensity; how they entice you, or goad you into reacting. When this happens, simply 'observe' them with the mind's eye as best you can. Remain curious about them. Often, the act of observing thoughts robs them of momentum and they simply melt away of their own accord. Whether this happens or not, after a few moments, return your awareness to the breath. After a few breaths, once again begin waiting patiently for a thought or emotion to arise in your mind. Allow them to appear in their own time.

8. If you feel an emotion – or an urge or impulse to do something – see if you can sense where it is located in the body. Feel the sensations rise and fall for a few moments and then return your awareness to the breath. After a few breaths, return to waiting patiently.

9. Try to gain a sense of what the absence of thoughts in your mind feels like … It might feel like a place of pure tranquillity, an 'emptiness' or perhaps of something vast just beyond your grasp. Be curious and open to what it feels like. Don't try to change anything. Whatever it seems like, simply wait patiently as if you are sitting on the edge of a vast pool.

10. The next time a thought or emotion arises, watch its rise and fall, return to the breath and then to patiently waiting and observing. You may run through this cycle a few times or perhaps ten or twenty times. It doesn't matter. Only awareness matters.

11. After five or six minutes, gradually shift the focus of your awareness to the world around you. What can you hear? … Gently open your eyes. Remain in this position for as long as you wish. When you do decide to move, begin by gently wiggling your fingers and toes before slowly getting out of your chair. See if you can maintain the essence of this clear and open awareness as you move through your day.

'Waiting for …'

At first Debbie found the Insight meditation immensely frustrating: 'The same thing would happen over and over again. My mind would become calm and I'd manage to find a gap in my thoughts. I'd focus on that gap for a few moments before my mind would take off again. I'd feel that I'd be getting somewhere and then it would all start to go wrong. It happened every time. It was so, so annoying.'

After a few attempts ending in abject frustration, Debbie began to realise why her meditation was 'going wrong': 'I'd found the first weeks of mindfulness to be rewarding. Sure, the meditations were sometimes a little tricky, but I always felt that I was getting somewhere, achieving something. I know you should not have a definite "aim" in mind when you meditate. I know that it's not about "success" or "failure", but deep down you need a reason to meditate, and for me the benefits were building quite nicely. I felt increasingly relaxed, I slept better and felt it easier to get into the flow of my work. So when it came to the Insight meditation I was expecting some kind of breakthrough. I'm not remotely spiritual, so I wasn't expecting some kind of "enlightenment" (whatever that would be), but I was expecting a better state of mind to appear. I expected to quickly develop great clarity of mind and purpose. I found an inkling of this. It felt as if they were there, just out of reach, just beyond my fingertips. It was so annoying to feel as if there was some kind of breakthrough that I couldn't quite make. So I got to the end of the week feeling very frustrated indeed.'

An apparent lack of concrete progress can be a major stumbling block for many who do the Insight meditation. If you look at the scientific evidence, then the benefits for creativity are clear, but that is not the same as instant. The human brain sadly does not work that way. Significant changes always take time. The benefits of the Insight meditation accrue in two stages. There is a definite increase in creativity in the hours that immediately follow the meditation, which is why it's best to do it in the morning. The hurly burly of daily life then begins to erode these gains. But not completely. This is because when you do the meditation the brain begins to reprogramme itself. Patterns of thought and behaviour that are used most commonly begin to wear tracks in the mind. Over time, the brain actually begins to rewire itself, so that these states are triggered more easily. So after a while, the clarity of mind and purpose cultivated by the Insight meditation becomes ever easier to trigger and tends to remain for longer.

Debbie followed the advice of her teacher, who reminded her that she should simply accept what she finds, no matter how initially frustrating that might feel. The teacher told her that once she accepted that the meditation can be difficult – and that the benefits might take a little time to accrue – that would, paradoxically, relieve some of the pressure that was driving her thoughts.

'I'd carried some of the ideas of "success" over to the Insight meditation. I put a little too much effort into focusing on the gaps in my thoughts. I began to almost "will" a thought into appearing, so that I could watch it and then return to focusing on the gap. It became almost a game where the object was to see the gap in my thoughts as fast as possible, and then to catch a thought, and return to the gap again. It was the opposite of patience.'

'Epiphany'

Like Debbie, Paul had expected something special to happen. But nothing did. Or at least it seemed that way – until one day, when he was in an editorial meeting at his newspaper office and he had a bit of an epiphany: 'I suddenly realised that I was working in a madhouse. I was calm and everyone else was virtually frothing at the mouth with stress, fear and anger.

'The editor was shouting at one of the feature editors for missing a story. Such aggressive behaviour is entirely normal at the paper, but that does not mean it had become "normalised". Everyone found his behaviour intolerable and stress was a major issue. It meant the whole editorial team were constantly watching their backs and living in fear – including me. I watched his behaviour and saw that the editor was also trapped by the system that he had helped to build. He was also working ridiculous hours and constantly chasing his own tail. He was almost a caricature of himself. He'd become like one of those deranged Roman emperors who'd become so paranoid that he could no longer think clearly or behave rationally. Oddly, I began to pity him and it dawned on me that I no longer needed him or the newspaper. I could also see through all of his bullying psychological tricks and understood that he only had control over me when I was frightened. Thing is, I just didn't feel frightened any more. It was like I'd been released from the mad storyline that the editor was weaving. As soon as I began to see the "story" from the outside, I was free. It no longer had any hold over me. It was an insight, I suppose.

'Later in the editorial meeting, when it was my turn to be attacked, I managed to allow his aggression to wash over me. I knew that in the long run I would need to leave the newspaper, but in the meantime all I had to do was remain calm and clear-sighted. I needed to focus on the gaps, to gain a sense of the way the tide was flowing, so that I could then exploit them by getting my favourite subjects and stories into the paper. Everyone else was in a blind and stressed state most of the time, so simply remaining calm enough to do my job gave me a huge advantage over the other journalists. Most of the staff, and my "competitors", spent so much time thinking in panicky and circular loops – or undermining each other – that simply focusing on my work as a feature writer gave me an edge. They fought like rats in a sack, while I came in, did my job, got important stories into the paper and went home. I had stepped outside of the editor's delusional loop. This meant that the quality of my work improved and that I began to enjoy it once again. The editor's ranting simply washed over me. In any case, I began to build a parallel life by concentrating on my fiction writing. Now I see my job as a means of paying off my debts and covering the mortgage until the money from my novels begins to flow. Even if I should fail as a novelist, at least I tried, which to me is the most important thing in the world.'

For an artist, 'flow' is the most elusive quality in the world. It so often lies just beyond reach – beyond the fingertips. Nora was a graphic artist for a style magazine. She was also struggling with her work and with her meditation. 'I was deeply, deeply tired,' she said. 'At first I thought it was the Insight meditation. Was it burning up too much energy? I'd been struggling for many months with my work. I just could not get into the right mental zone. I felt as if I was constantly off-course. As if I'd lost the path. I knew it was out there, somewhere, but just couldn't find it. I was doing an OK job, but not a great one. I wanted to do a brilliant one like I used to, which is why I turned to mindfulness.'

Nora found the first three weeks of the course a bit of a slog, but could see the benefits. The Insight meditation revealed a problem though. She was often too tired to maintain her concentration.

'Then I remembered what my meditation teacher said – that one of the "five hindrances" to mindfulness was mental tiredness (I think she used the phrase "sloth-torpor"). I didn't see this as a major problem in the first few weeks. I was tired, but I could cope because I'd always coped. The Insight meditation took this to a whole new level though. I think I'd been progressively calming down. I was no longer living off adrenaline. It felt like that moment when you pull off the motorway and take your foot off the accelerator and begin to slow down and then, all of a sudden, when you approach the junction you realise that you are still going way too fast. I realised that I was flying through life and not seeing the scenery. I was missing everything. That was why my work (and life) was suffering. I had nothing left to give. It took me weeks to begin picking myself up.'

Nora continued with the Insight meditation, even though she found it genuinely difficult. Each time her mind wandered she would scan her body and try to locate the centre of her tiredness. After exploring the tiredness for a while she would focus on the breath for a few moments and then return to waiting for her thoughts, feelings or emotions to begin bubbling up.

'The tiredness seemed to be located mostly in my head, around the top and back of it. It was really weird. A bone-deep tiredness. Almost like a pain. At other times it felt like my head was stuffed with cotton wool. It was deathly quiet, but not in a nice, calm and contemplative way. It was more like my brain had stopped working.

'I continued with the Insight meditation and I did eventually begin to regain my mental strength, but it was a long, slow haul. I did it mostly out of a sense of duty to myself. I did find my way back – primarily through sleep. God did I sleep! I had no idea I was so tired. I dreamed so much too. The dreams were incredibly vivid. For weeks, I'd wake up tired, but I could feel myself mending. It was a glorious feeling. Just feeling my energy creeping back was the most wonderful thing in the world. I'd always felt that momentum and adrenaline could make up for tiredness – that they would catapult me into the flow of my work. But, to be honest, a good night's sleep was far better!

'After I'd caught up on my sleep I started to notice more "coincidences". Chance meetings would kick-start ideas. Flicking through a magazine would start me thinking. Or perhaps I'd put together a collage of ideas that would somehow "just work". Just having the energy and clarity of mind and purpose to pursue ideas was of huge benefit to me. It's amazing how ideas drain away if you don't have the energy to pursue them. Equally, it's amazing how ideas keep appearing if you give them the confidence that you'll follow them through.'

HABIT RELEASERS

Choose one of the following two Habit Releasers and do it one day this week. As with last week, you can do both if you prefer.

Be naughty and spend thirty minutes less at work

How do you feel at the end of your working day? Shell-shocked and exhausted? Brain like cotton wool? Our 'long-hours culture' slowly burns out the mind, stifles creativity and is hopelessly inefficient . . . and yet few are willing to question the status quo. In fact, you'd be forgiven for thinking that our economy is geared towards maximising the amount of time spent *at* work with little regard to the end result. This is largely because our collective autopilot has locked in place inefficient and unhealthy work patterns. For this reason, this week's first Habit Releaser is to spend half an hour less at work.

If it's possible, try to leave work half an hour earlier or perhaps 'bunk off' for thirty minutes during the day. Alternatively, you can do it by taking your lunch hour in full. You should also remember not to check emails or answer any work-related calls (and if you don't recognise the number, don't answer it). However you do it, it is important that you do take this time off and spend it on yourself.

And how exactly should you spend this time? It's entirely up to you. You could use it to beat the rush hour home or perhaps meet a friend or partner for a drink or something to eat. You might like to go for a walk, read a book, rekindle an old hobby, take up a new one or perhaps write a letter to a friend (using pen and ink). If you're short of ideas, look at the Appendix on pages 181–8 for inspiration. The important thing is to do something 'unproductive' – not even remotely work-related – for the sheer hell of it. You might like to go and take some photos on your phone, go to an open space and watch the clouds drift past or watch the pigeons squabbling over a crust of bread. If your city is hilly, why not find the highest point and see it in a whole new light? If there's a river, go and watch the wildlife (you'll be surprised by how much there is to see if you stay still for a while). Alternatively, you could take a look at a noticeboard in your local library or community centre and see if any events take your fancy.

If you should start to feel a little guilty or even worried about your time away from work, remind yourself what countless studies have shown – that creativity, efficiency and productivity all increase when you spend less time at work. British people work the longest hours in Europe and yet our workers are among the least efficient. Americans aren't much better. Overwork is inextricably entwined with low productivity, and releasing yourself from its pressures allows your creative juices to flow.

It says a lot about our culture that doing 'naught' is considered 'naughty'.

Stop every two hours and soak up the world

Mindfulness is, at its heart, about being fully conscious of the world around you. Meditation is one way of doing this – but it's not the only way. To be truly mindful you need to integrate this state of awareness into your daily life. This Habit Releaser will help you do this by asking you to pause every two hours for twenty to thirty seconds while you pay full conscious attention to whatever you are doing. Treat it as a mini-meditation that helps you integrate mindfulness ever more closely into everyday life.

It's best if you use a timer on a watch or a phone for this exercise. Every two hours, pause and then focus on whatever you are doing and the thoughts, feelings and emotions flowing through your mind and body. Notice how they rise and fall and the way they tug at you to try to get you to engage with their story. If you can, close your eyes for a few moments and soak up any sounds, smells, tastes and textures. If you can't close your eyes, then pay full conscious attention to whatever you were looking at when the timer went off. Here are some pointers to look out for, whether your eyes are open or closed.

Examples of things you might become aware of:

• What can you see? Rather than seeing the scene as made up of a collection of discrete objects, see if you can pay attention to the scene as a whole. Soak it all up at once. Imagine your eyes and brain have become a panoramic camera. Once you have broadened your awareness in this way, shift your focus to one or two individual elements such as a chair, a window, or perhaps a car or tree. Pay attention to the different colours, shades, patterns and textures.

- What can you hear?

- What can you smell?

- What can you taste? Even the air has a taste. It may be stale or tinged with the flavour of greasy fast food or perhaps with the sweetness of flowers or grass or perhaps the 'buttery' taste of exhaust fumes.

- What textures can you feel with your fingers? Is there air flowing over your skin or through your hair? If you are sitting, can you feel the pressure where your legs and bottom touch the chair? How do your clothes feel on your skin? Can you feel your teeth? Nose? Feet? . . .

Remember that you don't need to spend long on this exercise, twenty to thirty seconds is enough. The aim is to reconnect with the world around you. If you can, try to maintain the essence of this exercise throughout the day, so that you become ever more connected to the world around you. Remember to reset the timer, so you can reconnect in two hours. Although you only need to do this Habit Releaser on one day, you can obviously repeat it as many times as you wish.

CHAPTER EIGHT

Neurogenesis

The final chapter of any 'self-help' book is normally a pep talk. Happiness and immense wealth will greet those (and only those) who have the gritty determination to follow the wise words of the author. It's a rousing call to arms which aims to catapult you into a bright future that only you can create for yourself. But this isn't a conventional self-help book. And you won't find any such final flourishes here.

Equally, the final chapter of many mindfulness books will encourage you to embrace a more 'meaningful' existence, one that is centred around lengthy daily meditations and a simpler, quieter and more harmonious life. Some may even urge you to go on regular meditation retreats lasting days or even weeks. But this is not a conventional meditation book either. You don't need one. You don't have any major problems that need 'fixing'. Nor, I suspect, are you seeking some form of spiritual enlightenment. Nevertheless, you will have begun to experience first-hand the benefits of mindfulness and are probably hoping for a distinct finale to this programme. But there isn't one. There couldn't be – because there is no precise destination to reach and definitely no right or wrong way to get there. This is because the final step in the programme is the rest of your life – and nobody knows how this will pan out (including, unfortunately, you).

You might find this sense of uncertainty a little unsatisfactory, but if you can instead learn to embrace it, then it opens up a radical new way of relating to the world. Instead of trying to make life less frustrating, and a little less uncertain, why not accept that it can never be so? Life is chaotic and full of unknowns. Distractions and surprises lie around every corner. It's a bit of a mess, really. But that's also what makes it interesting. Of course, this can also make it extremely difficult to remain focused, creative and mindful throughout the day – but with a little skill you can use the generalised chaos of daily life to facilitate your practice. For if you can begin to embrace the frantic world in which we all live – to use it as a meditation in itself – then it can become a source of mindful creativity.

But before you can do this, you need to get through the 'Week-Five blues', which will probably hit you right about now ...

In every mindfulness programme, people tend to become a little restless and despondent at Week Five. Nobody knows why. Even mindfulness texts from centuries past talk of maudlin thoughts that creep up on novice meditators and sap their energy. It might happen because the initial enthusiasm for meditation has begun to wane. Maybe it's the last gasp of certain negative habitual thoughts. Or perhaps the practices themselves have begun to unmask the fictions that we tell ourselves to get through the day.

Clarity can, after all, be a little unsettling. Whatever the reason, almost everyone will feel a little rudderless and occasionally unhappy after four or five weeks of meditation. But like everything else in life, it will pass.

The Week Five blues can take many forms, but rest assured they will feel absolutely real. They will have their own pattern that is unique to you, so their story will feel compelling and a fundamental part of you. You won't think, *Ah, this must be the Week-Five blues*, but rather things like, *Why am I bothering with this? . . . I'm useless . . . I can't do it . . . It's too hard . . . I don't have the time . . . What's the point? . . .* and so on.

Recognising that your enthusiasm for mindfulness has begun to wane is not a sign of failure. It is, instead, a sign of progress. And once you have noticed that this state of mind has crept up on you, then you can begin to take action; and you do this first by being gentle with yourself. So rather than criticising yourself for being weak or for 'failing' at meditation – or for not seeing the point of mindfulness – see if you can embrace such feelings. Be curious. Explore them. See them for what they are – memories; deeply buried stresses and strains rising to the surface; old patterns of thinking and behaving trying to reassert themselves; and passing mental events – rather than solid, objective truths about yourself and the world. Once these troubling states of mind have arisen, then you've crossed a watershed. You are then free to embrace this, the most important part of the programme: the rest of your life.

Although you've reached the end of the formal mindfulness programme, it is really just the beginning. Your brain may have spent decades wiring itself to think and behave in certain ways, so it will take more than four or five weeks of mindfulness to change your most entrenched thought patterns. Imagine turning around an oil tanker: at first nothing appears to happen, but gradually, as the miles pass, the ship changes its course. And it's the same with mindfulness. From day to day, little may appear to change, but when you look back and see how much more creative, decisive and happy you have become, then you realise that your life is in the process of being transformed. As this transformation gathers pace, your brain will rewire itself to embed the changes (it's known as neurogenesis). So over time the benefits of mindfulness will become a fundamental part of you, and your old 'negative' states of mind and approaches to life will have less and less control.

Nevertheless, if you wish to continue with this journey, you will need some very good reasons that resonate with your heart. After all, if you are to commit ten to twenty minutes a day to meditation, you will want to see significant ongoing benefits. Only you can decide if it is worth it. The scientific evidence is clear, but you may decide the benefits to you are not worth the investment of time. Or perhaps you might decide to take a sabbatical from mindfulness. However, most people who reach this point tend to continue and many of those who take a break tend to return when life once again begins to erode their emotional balance and clarity of mind.

If you do wish to continue, you should first try to clarify why, otherwise mindfulness will get squeezed out by seemingly higher priorities. So before you go any further, close your eyes and spend a few minutes examining *why* you might wish to continue. Allow each reason to slowly crystallise in your mind and to trigger other, deeper, reasons. You might hear mental echoes and longings. Or there may be logical reasons which might include:

- To remain calm and clear-sighted under pressure.

- To enhance creativity.

- To enhance mental focus.

- To make better decisions.

- To sleep better.

- To renew the courage necessary to follow your path through life.

- To enhance mental and physical resilience.

- To cope with the angst of making important decisions.

- To ward off, or relieve, anxiety, stress and unhappiness.

- To live a 'good' life that is meaningful and broadly happy.

Alternatively, you may not find a single purely logical reason, but simply have a feeling that you should continue. Both are equally valid.

If you do decide to continue, then you will need to begin building your own mindfulness programme that you can adapt day to day to fit your circumstances. Only you can know which will be the best practices to use each day. Just as each day is different, so the most appropriate meditation will vary. Some days you will feel lost, alone, vulnerable and defeated. At such times, the Resilience meditation will be there for you. On other days you might feel angry, stressed or unhappy. Life might have begun slipping through your fingers. The Breathing meditation was designed for such times. Sometimes you will feel strung out, lacking in focus and in desperate need of some mental peace and quiet. When this happens, the Sounds and Thoughts meditation will be best. (It's also useful for those busy times when you can't find enough peace and quiet to do the other practices – so you'll probably find yourself doing this one quite a lot.) And when you feel more or less on an even keel, then the Insight meditation will be the most fruitful. Whatever you feel each day, it will pay to spend a little time simply focusing on the breath. You will also find that the 90-Second Breathing Space will be invaluable in defusing stress before it becomes intolerable.

Bear in mind also that although the Insight meditation is best for enhancing creativity, in the long run, it will only do so if it is supported by the other techniques. For this reason, it makes sense to practise the Resilience and Breathing meditations at least once every week or two and the Insight meditation on the other days.

Regularity is important too. Even if you don't always manage it, it will pay to at least *aim* to meditate on five or six days per week at the same times each day. And as for how long – many people gravitate towards twenty minutes per day, while others find they gain far more by meditating for thirty minutes or even longer. Try to remember, though, any meditation is better than none, so even a few minutes of Breathing, or Sounds and Thoughts, will benefit you. As they say in yoga: 'The most difficult move is the one on to the mat.' You will also find it beneficial to do the meditations without following the tracks on the download: learning to meditate without external guidance is an important skill in its own right. And although you will find it best to stick to the four core practices, you might like to adapt them to suit your own requirements (see 'Mixing and matching meditations', pages 165–6).

And don't forget the power of changing your routines with

Habit Releasers. You will find a comprehensive list of extra ones in the Appendix (see pages 181–8). You can also repeat those you've already done, so long as you don't do them too often.

Mixing and matching meditations

Learning to guide your own meditations is an important skill. It allows you to create practices that suit your prevailing needs and moods. For example, if you feel annoyed, you might like to spend five minutes focusing on the breath, then do ten minutes of Resilience meditation, followed by five more minutes of Breathing meditation. Here are some other suggestions:

- **For acute stress:** a 90-Second Breathing Space.

- **When an immediate creative lift is needed:** a 90-Second Breathing Space, followed by 3 minutes of Insight meditation.

- **For making an important decision:** 2 minutes of focusing on the breath, followed by 3 of Insight meditation.

- **For anxiety, stress or unhappiness:** 10 minutes of Breathing followed by 10 minutes of Resilience, finishing off with 5–10 minutes of Breathing

- **When struggling with anger, bitterness or hate:** 10 minutes of Breathing followed by 10 of Resilience then 10 minutes of Insight.

- **When preparing for the gym or a run, etc.:** 5 minutes of Breathing (and perhaps try to do the exercises with full mindful awareness), finishing off with 5 minutes of Breathing.

- **When travelling or where there is nowhere to meditate:** Sounds and Thoughts for 10–20 minutes.

- **No time to meditate:** focus on whatever you are doing. For example, if you are eating or drinking, adapt the Coffee meditation to suit. If you are stuck in a queue, observe your reactions. The possibilities are endless …

It is important to decide which meditation you will do *before* you start, otherwise you will kick-start the mind's Doing mode and may well end up spending your time thinking about the best meditation to practise, rather than actually doing it. Equally, any meditation is better than none, so try not to spend too much time deciding. You might like to download a meditation timer app for your phone. Many people use the Insight Timer by Spotlight Six Software.

LIFE (AND CHAOS) AS MEDITATION

This book has taught you a series of meditations that can transform your life. But the truth is, they all pale into insignificance when faced with the most powerful meditation of all: your life. Creativity is the art of noticing. It is noticing the world around you in all of its frantic turmoil. It's being fully aware of your own emotions and the new ideas streaming through your mind. It is noticing – and embracing – your darkest moments with the same warmth and courage with which you greet your happiest hours. It is simply paying attention to your life as it *actually* happens. And the meditations that you have learned here are the tools – scaffolding, really – that help you to do all this.

As you've worked your way through this book you will have come to realise that mindfulness is not about trying to clear your mind of thoughts. It is not about peace and quiet, about sitting on cushions in meditation retreats, or about a simple life lived in simple surroundings. It is about embracing life by becoming fully conscious and aware as you pass through your day – being in touch with absolutely everything that is going on around you and inside you. It is about the noisy kids interrupting your meditation, the car horns in the distance, doors slamming, cats yowling and dogs barking. But most of all, it is about the noise and turmoil of your own mind. So go ahead – meditate in the wind and the rain, on noisy buses and trains, in the hurly burly of cafés, bars and restaurants. Wherever you find madness, chaos and anarchy, embrace them all as meditations. And when you do so, you will gain true insight.

NOTES

CHAPTER ONE: HOLE IN THE HEAD

1. Colzato, L. S., Ozturk, A. and Hommel, B. (2012), 'Meditate to create: the impact of focused-attention and open-monitoring training on convergent and divergent thinking', *Frontiers in Psychology*, 3:116, doi: 10.3389/fpsyg.2012.00116; Greenberg, J., Reiner, K. and Meiran, N. (2012), '"Mind the trap": mindfulness practice reduces cognitive rigidity', *PLoS One*, 7(5): e36206, doi: 10.1371/ journal. pone.0036206; Capurso, V., Fabbro, F. and Crescentini, C. (2014), 'Mindful creativity: the influence of mindfulness meditation on creative thinking', *Frontiers in Psychology*, 4:1020, doi: 10.3389/ fpsyg.2013.01020.
2. Jha, A., Krompinger, J. and Baime, M. J. (2007), 'Mindfulness training modifies subsystems of attention', *Cognitive Affective and Behavioral Neuroscience*, 7, pp. 109–19; Tang, Y. Y., Ma, Y., Wang, J., Fan, Y., Feng, S. and Lu, Q. (2007), 'Short-term meditation training improves attention and self- regulation', *Proceedings of the National Academy of Sciences of the United States of America*, 104(43), pp. 17152–6; Zeidan, F., Johnson, S. K., Diamond, B. J., David, Z. and Goolkasian, P. (2010), 'Mindfulness meditation improves cognition: evidence of brief mental training', *Consciousness and Cognition*, 19(2), pp. 597–605; McCracken, L. M. and Yang, S. Y. (2008), 'A contextual cognitive–behavioral analysis of rehabilitation workers' health and well-being: influences

of acceptance, mindfulness and values-based action', *Rehabilitation Psychology*, 53, pp. 479–85; Ortner, C. N. M., Kilner, S. J. and Zelazo, P. D. (2007), 'Mindfulness meditation and reduced emotional interference on a cognitive task', *Motivation and Emotion*, 31, pp. 271–83; Brefczynski-Lewis, J. A., Lutz, A., Schaefer, H. S., Levinson, D. B. and Davidson, R. J. (2007), 'Neural correlates of attentional expertise in long-term meditation practitioners', *Proceedings of the National Academy of Sciences of the United States of America*, 104(27), pp. 11483–8.

3. Hafenbrack, A. C., Kinias, Z. and Barsade, S. G. (2014), 'Debiasing the mind through meditation: mindfulness and the sunk-cost bias', *Psychological Science*, 25(2), p. 369; Hooria, J. (2014), 'Can mindfulness improve decision making?', Greater Good Science Center (University of California, Berkeley), at http://bit.ly/QMVF28.

4. Hölzel, B. K., Ott, U., Gard, T., Hempel, H., Weygandt, M., Morgen, K. and Vaitl, D. (2008), 'Investigation of mindfulness meditation practitioners with voxel-based morphometry', *Social Cognitive and Affective Neuroscience*, 3, pp. 55–61; Lazar, S., Kerr, C., Wasserman, R., Gray, J., Greve, D., Treadway, M., McGarvey, M., Quinn, B., Dusek, J., Benson, H., Rauch, S., Moore, C. and Fischl, B. (2005), 'Meditation experience is associated with increased cortical thickness', *NeuroReport*, 16, pp. 1893–7; Luders, E., Toga, A. W., Lepore, N. and Gaser, C. (2009), 'The underlying anatomical correlates of long-term meditation: larger hippocampal and frontal volumes of gray matter', *Neuroimage*, 45, pp. 672–8.

5. Tang, Y., Ma, Y., Wang, J., Fan, Y., Feng, S., Lu, Q., Yu, Q., Sui, D., Rothbart, M., Fan, M. and Posner, M. (2007), 'Short-term meditation training improves attention and self-regulation', *Proceedings of the National Academy of Sciences of the United States of America*, 104, pp. 17152–6.

6. Davidson, R. J. (2004), 'Well-being and affective style: neural substrates and biobehavioural correlates', *Philosophical Transactions of the Royal Society*, 359, pp. 1395–411.

7. Lazar, S., Kerr, C., Wasserman, R., Gray, J., Greve, D., Treadway, M., McGarvey, M., Quinn, B., Dusek, J., Benson, J., Rauch, S., Moore, C. and Fischl, B. (2005), 'Meditation experience is associated with increased cortical thickness', *NeuroReport*, 16, pp. 1893–7.

8. Ivanowski, B. and Malhi, G. S. (2007), 'The psychological and

neurophysiological concomitants of mindfulness forms of meditation', *Acta Neuropsychiatrica*, 19, pp. 76–91; Shapiro, S. L., Oman, D., Thoresen, C. E., Plante, T. G. and Flinders, T. (2008), 'Cultivating mindfulness: effects on well-being', *Journal of Clinical Psychology*, 64(7), pp. 840–62; Shapiro, S. L., Schwartz, G. E. and Bonner, G. (1998), 'Effects of mindfulness-based stress reduction on medical and pre-medical students', *Journal of Behavioral Medicine*, 21, pp. 581–99.

9. See 'Depression in adults: The treatment and management of depression in adults', NICE clinical guideline 90, issued October 2009; Ma, J. and Teasdale, J. D. (2004), 'Mindfulness-Based Cognitive Therapy for depression: replication and exploration of differential relapse prevention effects', *Journal of Consulting and Clinical Psychology*, 72, pp. 31–40; Segal, Z. V., Williams, J. M. G. and Teasdale, J. D. (2002), *Mindfulness-Based Cognitive Therapy for Depression: A New Approach to Preventing Relapse* (New York: Guilford Press); Kenny, M. A. and Williams, J. M. G. (2007), 'Treatment-resistant depressed patients show a good response to Mindfulness-Based Cognitive Therapy', *Behaviour Research and Therapy*, 45, pp. 617–25; Eisendraeth, S. J., Delucchi, K., Bitner, R., Fenimore, P., Smit, M. and McLane, M. (2008), 'Mindfulness-Based Cognitive Therapy for treatment-resistant depression: a pilot study', *Psychotherapy and Psychosomatics*, 77, pp. 319–20; Kingston, T., Dooley, B., Bates, A., Lawlor, E. and Malone, K. (2007), 'Mindfulness-Based Cognitive Therapy for residual depressive symptoms', *Psychology and Psychotherapy*, 80(2), pp. 193–203.

10. Davidson, R. J., Kabat-Zinn, J., Schumacher, J., Rosenkranz, M., Muller, D., Santorelli, S. F., Urbanowski, F., Harrington, A., Bonus, K. and Sheridan, J. F. (2003), 'Alterations in brain and immune function produced by mindfulness meditation', *Psychosomatic Medicine*, 65, pp. 564–70; Tang, Y., Ma, Y., Wang, J., Fan, Y., Feng, S., Lu, Q., Yu, Q., Sui, D., Rothbart, M., Fan, M. and Posner, M. (2007), 'Short-term meditation training improves attention and self-regulation', *Proceedings of the National Academy of Sciences of the United States of America*, 104, pp. 17152–6.

11. Walsh, R. and Shapiro, S. L. (2006), 'The meeting of meditative disciplines and Western psychology: a mutually enriching dialogue', *American Psychologist*, 61, pp. 227–39.

12. Zeidan, F., Martucci, K. T., Kraft, R. A., Gordon, N. S., McHaffie,

J. G. and Coghill, R. C. (2011), 'Brain mechanisms supporting the modulation of pain by mindfulness meditation', *Journal of Neuroscience*, 31(14), pp. 5540–8.

13. Neal, D. T., Wood, W. and Quinn, J. M. (2006), 'Habits: a repeat performance', *Current Directions in Psychological Science*, 15(4), pp. 198–202; Verplanken, B. and Wood, W. (2006), 'Interventions to break and create consumer habits', *Journal of Public Policy and Marketing*, 25(1), pp. 90–103.

14. Fredrickson, B. L., Cohn, M. A., Coffey, K. A., Pek, J. and Finkel, S. M. (2008), 'Open hearts build lives: positive emotions, induced through loving-kindness meditation, build consequential personal resources', *Journal of Personality and Social Psychology*, 95, pp. 1045–62; see Barbara Fredrickson's website at http://www.unc. edu/peplab/home.html.

CHAPTER TWO: SERENDIPITY

1. Jha, A. P., Stanley, E. A., Kiyonaga, A., Wong, L. and Gelfand, L. (2010), 'Examining the protective effects of mindfulness training on working memory capacity and affective experience', *Emotion*, 10, pp. 54–64; Jha, A. P., Krompinger, J. and Baime, M. J. (2007), 'Mindfulness training modifies subsystems of attention', *Cognitive, Affective and Behavioral Neuroscience*, 7, pp. 109–19; Johnson, D. C., Thom, N. J., Stanley, E. A., Haase, L., Simmons, A. N., Shih, P. B., Thompson, W. K., Potterat, E. G., Minor, T. R. and Paulus, M. P. (2014), 'Modifying resilience mechanisms in at-risk individuals: a controlled study of mindfulness training in Marines preparing for deployment', *American Journal of Psychiatry*, 171, pp. 844–53.

2. Gunnery Sergeant Chris Dixon has now retired from the US Marines and is training to teach Mindfulness-based Mind Fitness Training (a mindfulness programme adapted for use on the battlefield and in other high-stress situations) to various branches of the US military. See http://www.mind-fitness-training.org/training.html.

3. See https://www.creativityatwork.com/2014/02/17/what-is-creativity/.

4. See http://en.wikipedia.org/wiki/Convergent_thinking; Cropley, A. (2006), 'In praise of convergent thinking', *Creativity Research Journal*, 18(3), pp. 391–404.

5. Hanson, R. (2009), *Buddha's Brain: The Practical Neuroscience of Happiness, Love and Wisdom* (Oakland, CA: New Harbinger

Publications). See also 'Session 1: How the Mind Changes the Brain', *The Compassionate Brain* audio series, at http://www.SoundsTrue. com (interview between Dr Rick Hanson and Dr Richard Davison).

6. For a good overview, see Gilbert, P. (2009), *The Compassionate Mind* (London: Constable and Robinson): ch. 2.

7. Reb, J., Narayanan, J. and Chaturvedi, S. (2014), 'Leading mindfully: two studies on the influence of supervisor trait mindfulness on employee well-being and performance', *Mindfulness*, 5(1), pp. 36–45.

8. Friedman, R. S. and Forster, J. (2001), 'The effects of promotion and prevention cues on creativity', *Journal of Personality and Social Psychology*, 81, pp. 1001–13; adapted from Williams, M. and Penman, D. (2011), *Mindfulness: A Practical Guide to Finding Peace in a Frantic World* (London: Piatkus).

9. Karelaia, N. (2014), 'Why mindful individuals make better decisions', INSEAD Knowledge, 23 July, at http://knowledge. insead. edu/leadership-management/why-mindful-individuals-make-better-decisions-3479.

10. Hafenbrack, A. C., Kinias, Z. and Barsade, S. G. (2014), 'Debiasing the mind through meditation: mindfulness and the sunk-cost bias', *Psychological Science*, 25(2), pp. 369–76.

11. Mrazek, M. D., Franklin, M. S., Phillips, D. T., Baird, B. and Schooler, J. W. (2013), 'Mindfulness training improves working memory capacity and GRE performance while reducing mind wandering', *Psychological Science*, 24, pp. 776–81; Jha, A. P., Stanley, E. A., Kiyonaga, A., Wong, L. and Gelfand, L. (2010), 'Examining the protective effects of mindfulness training on working memory capacity and affective experience', *Emotion*, 10, pp. 54–64; Jha, A. P., Krompinger, J. and Baime, M. J. (2007), 'Mindfulness training modifies subsystems of attention', *Cognitive, Affective and Behavioral Neuroscience*, 7, pp. 109–19; Zeidan, F., Johnson, S. K., Diamond, B. J., David, Z. and Goolkasian, P. (2010), 'Mindfulness meditation improves cognition: evidence of brief mental training', *Consciousness and Cognition*, 19(2), pp. 597–605.

12. Zeidan, F., Johnson, S. K., Diamond, B. J., David, Z. and Goolkasian, P. (2010), 'Mindfulness meditation improves cognition: evidence of brief mental training', *Consciousness and Cognition*, 19(2), pp. 597–605; Greenberg, J., Reiner, K. and Meiran, N. (2012), '"Mind the trap": mindfulness practice reduces cognitive rigidity', *PLoS One*, 7(5): e36206, doi:10.1371/ journal.pone.0036206

13. Hafenbrack, A. C., Kinias, Z. and Barsade, S. G. (2014), 'Debiasing the mind through meditation: mindfulness and the sunk-cost bias', *Psychological Science*, 25(2), p. 369; Kirk, U., Downar, J. and Montague, P. R. (2011), 'Interoception drives increased rational decision-making in meditators playing the ultimatum game', *Frontiers in Neuroscience*, 5:49, doi: 10.3389/ fnins.2011.00049.

14. Ostafin, B. and Kassman, K. (2012), 'Stepping out of history: mindfulness improves insight problem solving', *Consciousness and Cognition*, 21(2), pp. 1031–6.

15. Neal D. T., Wood, W. and Quinn, J. M. (2006), 'Habits: a repeat performance', *Current Directions in Psychological Science*, 15(4) pp. 198–202; Verplanken, B. and Wood, W. (2006), 'Interventions to break and create consumer habits', *Journal of Public Policy and Marketing*, 25(1), pp. 90–103. For a good overview of the field, see Fletcher, B. C., Pine, K. and Penman, D. (2005), *The No Diet Diet* (London: Orion); see also Duhigg, C. (2012), *The Power of Habit* (New York: Random House).

17416.   For an overview, see Banich, M. T. and Compton, R. (2010), *Cognitive Neuroscience*, 3rd edition (Boston, MA: Cengage Learning): p. 118.

17. Way, B. M., Creswell, J. D., Eisenberger, N. I. and Lieberman, M. D. (2010), 'Dispositional mindfulness and depressive symptomatol-ogy: correlations with limbic and self-referential neural activity during rest', *Emotion*, 10, pp. 12–24.

18. Mockenhaupt, B. (2012), 'A state of military mind', *Pacific Standard*, 18 June, at http://www.psmag.com/health/a-state-military-mind-42839.

19. Segal, Z. V., Williams, J. M. G. and Teasdale, J. (2002), *Mindfulness-Based Cognitive Therapy for Depression: A New Approach to Preventing Relapse* (New York: Guilford Press): p. 70.

20. Segal, Z. V., Williams, J. M. G. and Teasdale, J. (2002), *Mindfulness-Based Cognitive Therapy for Depression: A New Approach to Preventing Relapse* (New York: Guilford Press): p. 73.

21. Williams, M., Teasdale, J., Segal, Z. V. and Kabat-Zinn, J. (2007), *The Mindful Way through Depression* (New York: Guilford Press): p. 47; see also Williams, M. and Penman, D. (2011), *Mindfulness: A Practical Guide to Finding Peace in a Frantic World* (London: Piatkus): p. 35.

CHAPTER FOUR: WEEK ONE: ADAPT

1. Langer, E. J. (2014), personal communication; see also the excellent Langer, E. J. (1989), *Mindfulness* (Boston, MA: a Merloyd Lawrence book by Da Capo Press): p. 2.

2. Adapted from the 'Coffee Meditation' in Penman, D. and Burch, V. (2013), *Mindfulness for Health: A Practical Guide to Relieving Pain, Reducing Stress and Restoring Wellbeing* (London: Piatkus): pp. 51–2.

3. See Penman, D. and Burch, V. (2013), *Mindfulness for Health: A Practical Guide to Relieving Pain, Reducing Stress and Restoring Wellbeing* (London: Piatkus): p. 159.

4. Carney, D. R., Cuddy, A. J. and Yap, A. J. (2010), 'Power posing brief nonverbal displays affect neuroendocrine levels and risk tolerance', *Psychological Science*, 21(10), pp. 1363–8.

5. Slepian, M. L., Weisbuch, M., Rule, N. O. and Ambady, N. (2011), 'Tough and tender: embodied categorization of gender', *Psychological Science*, 22(1), pp. 26–8.

6. Strack, F., Martin, L. and Stepper, S. (1988), 'Inhibiting and facilitating conditions of the human smile: a nonobtrusive test of the facial feedback hypothesis', *Journal of Personality and Social Psychology*, 54, pp. 768–77.

7. Danziger, S., Levav, J. and Avnaim-Pesso, L. (2011), 'Extraneous factors in judicial decisions', *Proceedings of the National Academy of Sciences of the United States of America*, 108(17), pp. 6889–92; see also Corbyn, Z. (2011), 'Hungry judges dispense rough justice', 11 April, at http://www.nature.com/news/2011/110411/full/news.2011.227.html.

CHAPTER FIVE: WEEK TWO: CREATE

1. Ostafin, B. D. and Kassman, K. T. (2012), 'Stepping out of history: mindfulness improves insight problem solving', *Consciousness and Cognition*, 21, pp. 1031–6.

2. Schooler, J. W., Ohlsson, S. and Brooks, K. (1993), 'Thoughts beyond words: when language overshadows insight', *Journal of Experimental Psychology: General*, 122, pp. 166–83.

3. Greenberg, J., Reiner, K. and Meiran, N. (2012) '"Mind the trap": mindfulness practice reduces cognitive rigidity', *PLoS One*, 7(5): e36206, doi: 10.1371/journal.pone.0036206.

4. Ibid.

5. Ostafin, B. D. and Kassman, K. T. (2012) 'Stepping out of history: mindfulness improves insight problem solving', *Consciousness and Cognition*, 21, pp. 1031–6.

6. Ostafin, B. D. (2014), personal communication.

7. Colzato, L. S., Ozturk, A. and Hommel, B. (2012) 'Meditate to create: the impact of focused-attention and open-monitoring training on convergent and divergent thinking', *Frontiers in Psychology*, 3:116, doi: 10.3389/fpsyg.2012.00116; Capurso, V., Fabbro, F. and Crescentini, C. (2014), 'Mindful creativity: the influence of mindfulness meditation on creative thinking', *Frontiers in Psychology*, 4:1020, doi: 10.3389/fpsyg.2013.01020; see also Colzato, L. S., Szapora, A., Lippelt, D. and Hommel, B. (2014), 'Prior meditation practice modulates performance and strategy use in convergent- and divergent-thinking problems', *Mindfulness*, 29 October, doi: 10.1007/s12671-014-0352-9.

8. Zeidan, F., Johnson, S. K., Diamond, B. J., David, Z. and Goolkasian, P. (2010), 'Mindfulness meditation improves cognition: evidence of brief mental training', *Consciousness and Cognition*, 19(2), pp. 597–605.

9. Colzato, L. S., Szapora, A., Lippelt, D. and Hommel, B. (2014), 'Prior meditation practice modulates performance and strategy use in convergent- and divergent-thinking problems', *Mindfulness*, 29 October, doi: 10.1007/s12671-014-0352-9.

10. Gilbert, P. (2010), *The Compassionate Mind*, paperback edition (London: Constable and Robinson): p. 34.

11. Adapted from Mark Williams's 'Sounds and Thoughts Meditation': see Williams, M. and Penman, D. (2011), *Mindfulness: A Practical Guide to Finding Peace in a Frantic World* (London: Piatkus): pp. 143–6. This meditation is based on Kabat-Zinn, J. (1990), *Full Catastrophe Living: Using the Wisdom of Your Body and Mind to Face Stress, Pain and Illness* (London: Piatkus) and Williams, J. M. G, Teasdale, J. D., Segal, Z. V. and Kabat-Zinn, J. (2007), *The Mindful Way through Depression: Freeing Yourself from Chronic Unhappiness* (New York: Guilford Press).

12. Ibid.

13. Based on the concept of the 'Three-minute Breathing Space' used in Mindfulness-Based Cognitive Therapy (MBCT): see Segal, Z.

V., Williams, J. M.G. and Teasdale, J. (2002), *Mindfulness-Based Cognitive Therapy for Depression: A New Approach to Preventing Relapse* (New York: Guilford Press): p. 184.

14. Oppezzo, M. and Schwartz, D. L. (2014), 'Give your ideas some legs: the positive effect of walking on creative thinking', *Journal of Experimental Psychology: Learning, Memory, and Cognition*, 40(4), pp. 1142–52.

CHAPTER SIX: WEEK THREE: RESILIENCE

1. Fredrickson, B. L., Cohn, M. A., Coffey, K. A., Pek, J. and Finkel, S. M. (2008), 'Open hearts build lives: positive emotions, induced through loving-kindness meditation, build consequential personal resources', *Journal of Personality and Social Psychology*, 95, pp. 1045–62; see Barbara Fredrickson's website at http://www.unc.edu/peplab/home.html.

2. Often translated from the original Pali as 'loving-kindness'.

3. Fredrickson, B. L., Cohn, M. A., Coffey, K. A., Pek, J. and Finkel, S. M. (2008), 'Open hearts build lives: positive emotions, induced through loving-kindness meditation, build consequential personal resources', *Journal of Personality and Social Psychology*, 95, pp. 1045–62; see Barbara Fredrickson's website at http://www.unc.edu/peplab/home.html.

4. Colzato, L. S., Szapora, A., Lippelt, D. and Hommel, B. (2012), 'Prior meditation practice modulates performance and strategy use in convergent- and divergent-thinking problems', *Mindfulness*, 29 October, doi: 10.1007/s12671-014-0352-9.

5. Shahar, B., Szsepsenwol, O., Zilcha-Mano, S., Haim, N., Zamir, O., Levi-Yeshuvi, S. and Levit-Binnun, N. (2014), 'A wait-list randomized controlled trial of loving-kindness meditation programme for self-criticism', *Clinical Psychology and Psychotherapy*, 16 March, doi: 10.1002/cpp.1893.

6. Walsh, R. and Shapiro, S. L. (2006), 'The meeting of meditative disciplines and Western psychology: a mutually enriching dialogue', *American Psychologist*, 61, pp. 227–39.

7. Epel, E., Daubenmier, J., Moskowitz, J. T., Folkman, S. and Blackburn, E. (2009), 'Can meditation slow rate of cellular aging? Cognitive stress, mindfulness, and telomeres', *Annals of the New York Academy of Sciences*, 1172, pp. 34–53; Hoge, E. A., Chen, M.

M., Orr, E., Metcalf, C. A., Fischer, L. E., Pollack, M. H., De Vivo, I. and Simon, N. M. (2013), 'Loving-kindness meditation practice associated with longer telomeres in women', *Brain, Behavior, and Immunity*, 32, pp. 159–63.

8. Hutcherson, C. A., Seppala, E. M. and Gross, J. J. (2015), 'The neural correlates of social connection', *Cognitive, Affective and Behavioral Neuroscience*, 15(1), pp. 1–14; Hofmann, S. G., Grossman, P. and Hinton, D. E. (2011), 'Loving-kindness and compassion meditation: potential for psychological interventions', *Clinical Psychology Review*, 31(7), pp. 1126–32; Leung, M. K., Chan, C. C., Yin, J., Lee, C. F., So, K. F. and Lee, T. M. (2013), 'Increased gray matter volume in the right angular and posterior parahippocampal gyri in loving-kindness meditators', *Social Cognitive and Affective Neuroscience*, 8(1), pp. 34–9; Lutz, A., Brefczynski-Lewis, J., Johnstone, T. and Davidson, R. J. (2008), 'Regulation of the neural circuitry of emotion by compassion meditation: effects of meditative expertise', *PLoS One*, 3(3): e1897, doi: 10.1371/journal.pone.0001897; Lee, T. M., Leung, M. K., Hou, W. K., Tang, J. C., Yin, J., So, K. F., Lee, C. F. and Chan, C. C. (2012), 'Distinct neural activity associated with focused-attention meditation and loving-kindness meditation', *PLoS One*, 7(8): e40054, doi: 10.1371/journal.pone.0040054. For an overview, see also Seppälä, E. (2014), '18 science-based reasons to try loving-kindness meditation', at http://www.mindful.org/mindfulness-practice/18-science- based-reasons-to-try-loving-kindness-meditation.

9. Leung, M. K., Chan, C. C., Yin, J., Lee, C. F., So, K. F. and Lee, T. M. (2013), 'Increased gray matter volume in the right angular and posterior parahippocampal gyri in loving-kindness meditators', *Social Cognitive and Affective Neuroscience*, 8(1), pp. 34–9; Lutz, A., Brefczynski-Lewis, J., Johnstone, T. and Davidson, R. J. (2008), 'Regulation of the neural circuitry of emotion by compassion meditation: effects of meditative expertise', *PLoS One*, 3(3): e1897, doi: 10.1371/journal.pone.0001897; Lee, T. M., Leung, M. K., Hou, W. K., Tang, J. C., Yin, J., So, K. F., Lee, C. F. and Chan, C. C. (2012), 'Distinct neural activity associated with focused-attention meditation and loving-kindness meditation', *PLoS One*, 7(8): e40054, doi: 10.1371/journal.pone.0040054.

10. Shahar, B., Szsepsenwol, O., Zilcha-Mano, S., Haim, N., Zamir, O., Levi-Yeshuvi, S. and Levit-Binnun, N. (2014), 'A wait-list randomized controlled trial of loving-kindness meditation programme for

self-criticism', *Clinical Psychology and Psychotherapy*, 16 March, doi: 10.1002/cpp.1893.

11. As examples: Cohen, P. (2001), 'Mental gymnastics increase bicep strength', *New* Scientist, 21 November, at http://www.newscientist. com/article/dn1591-mental-gymnastics-increase-bicep-strength. html; Ranganathan, V. K., Siemionow, V., Liu, J. Z., Sahgal, V. and Yue, G. H. (2004), 'From mental power to muscle power: gaining strength by using the mind', *Neuropsychologia*, 42(7), pp. 944–56.

12. See Langer, E. J. (2005), *On Becoming an Artist: Reinventing Yourself through Mindful Creativity* (New York: Ballantine Books): p. 54.

CHAPTER SEVEN: WEEK FOUR: INSIGHT

1. Colzato, L. S., Ozturk, A. and Hommel, B. (2012), 'Meditate to create: the impact of focused-attention and open-monitoring training on convergent and divergent thinking', *Frontiers in Psychology*, 3:116, doi: 10.3389/fpsyg.2012.00116; Capurso, V., Fabbro, F. and Crescentini, C. (2014), 'Mindful creativity: the influence of mindfulness meditation on creative thinking', *Frontiers in Psychology*, 4:1020, doi: 10.3389/fpsyg.2013.01020; see also Colzato, L. S., Szapora, A., Lippelt, D. and Hommel, B. (2014), 'Prior meditation practice modulates performance and strategy use in convergent- and divergent-thinking problems', *Mindfulness*, 29 October, doi: 10.1007/s12671-014-0352-9.

APPENDIX

1. Catmull, E., *Creativity, Inc.: Overcoming the Unseen Forces That Stand in the Way of True Inspiration* (hardcover, Bantam Press, 2014).

HABIT RELEASERS

Habit Releasers are a very effective way of enhancing creativity. Here are some more ideas.

Switch table and chairs at a meeting

Ed Catmull, co-founder of Pixar Animation, tells a story about how they overcame a series of inexplicable creative blocks while making *Toy Story 2*, among other films [1] Ed and his team of creatives regularly met around a long, elegant table crafted by one of Steve Jobs' favourite designers (Jobs provided the founding capital for Pixar and was a great cheerleader for the company).

'I grew to hate this table,' says Ed. 'It was long and skinny, like one of those things you'd see in a comedy sketch about an old, wealthy couple that sits down for dinner – one person at either end, a candelabra in the middle – and has to shout to make conversation.'

For purely practical reasons, Ed and his director and producer would sit in the middle. The main creative officers would then sit around them and the rest of the team would be seated even further out. To keep the seating organised, someone created place cards.

'When it comes to creative inspiration, job titles and hierarchy are meaningless,' says Ed. 'But, unwittingly, we were allowing this table – and the resulting place-card ritual – to send a different message. The closer you were seated to the middle of the table, it implied, the more important – the more central – you must be. And the farther away, the less likely you were to speak up – your distance from the heart of the conversation made participating feel intrusive ... Without intending to, we'd created an obstacle that discouraged people from jumping in.

'It wasn't until we happened to have a meeting in a smaller room with a square table that John [the director of the movie] and I realised what was wrong. Sitting around that table, the interplay was better, the exchange of ideas more free-flowing, the eye contact automatic. Every person there, no matter their job title, felt free to speak up. This was not only what we wanted, it was a fundamental Pixar belief: unhindered communication was key, no matter what your position.'

Shortly after this, one of Pixar's directors, Andrew Stanton, went further by randomly allocating seating by mixing up the place cards. That further enhanced the exchange of ideas. The place cards were thrown away soon after, so that everyone could choose for themselves where to sit.

Ed Catmull had unwittingly created a series of habits that hindered free-flowing creativity. And we all do it every day. Every time you meet at the same place, sit at the same table, in the same chair, you subtly reinforce the web of habits associated with that place.

Without realising it, you slip into habitual ways of thinking and approaching problems – a style that hampers creativity and impairs effective decision making.

One day this week, each time you go to a meeting or visit a familiar pub or café with friends, see if you can notice the subtle pull of habits guiding you to a specific table and chair. Try choosing a different one. Is it strangely difficult to do so? Does your mind come up with reasons why you should choose the familiar over the unfamiliar? Thoughts such as *It's less crowded down that end of the table*, or *The light's better over there*, or *It just feels more comfortable over there* might crop up. Such rationales allow habits to thrive, so you can easily lose the personal interplay that drives creativity. Hierarchies can be reinforced and politics can emerge. But simply moving chairs can alter the whole creative dynamic. Try, if you can, changing meeting rooms entirely or hold one in a café, restaurant or pub. The more unfamiliar the environment, the more the old barriers to creativity will break down.

Contact an old friend or distant family member

The hectic busyness of daily life can make it difficult to stay in day-to-day contact with family and friends. Social media can help, but we are physical, not virtual, creatures, so personal contact is still needed if you want to truly thrive. Having a wide circle of friends is good for creativity too, as it broadens the diversity of opinions and ideas you are exposed to. Serendipity plays its part as well. For these reasons (and out of sheer curiosity), why not phone someone you haven't contacted for a while?

The aim of this Habit Releaser is to re-establish contact with someone you've drifted away from, rather than consciously severed ties with. You needn't feel obliged to phone someone you haven't spoken to for twenty years, although you can do if you want to. If there is someone you've been keen to contact for many years – say, an old school or college friend, colleague or former neighbour – but feel a little self-conscious about doing so, then you can first send them an email or social-media 'friend' request to test the waters. The precise method you use to arrange a phone call is not that important. You could even write or send a postcard. It might feel a little awkward at first, but this will quickly pass.

If they don't respond, try to remember that there may be many reasons for this, so don't automatically assume you've been snubbed. They might be too busy to respond immediately (preferring to do so with more thought at a later date) or they may have missed your message entirely or been swept along by other things. Why not try again in a week or two?

Redesign – or mix up – your workspace

Most people are so familiar with their office, desk or studio that they barely notice it at all. But an overly familiar workspace can steer you down creative blind alleys and progressively fossilise the mind. This is because every object in your life acts as a mental filing cabinet full of triggers for memories and habitual thought patterns. The smell of a lover's perfume, an old photograph or a holiday souvenir can all transport you instantly to a different time and place. If you have worked in the same place for a while, then virtually everything will have become overlaid with mental triggers that encourage you to think along the same old, familiar lines.

In practice this means that if you want to change the way that you think, you can start by simply changing your environment. And a good place to begin is with your personal workspace. If it is a little untidy and cluttered, then spend fifteen minutes tidying it up. If it's tidy and 'minimalist', then spend the same time rearranging it, so that it's slightly less ordered. It might be worth bringing in a few books, newspapers or personal mementos to make it less pristine-looking. Change is the key to this exercise: there is no single 'best' way of rearranging your world, so simply aim to change it.

It's important to carry out this exercise mindfully, to pay full conscious attention to what you are doing. For example, if you tidy up a pile of paper, pay attention to what it feels like. Is the paper smooth, crinkly or rough? Thick or thin? Stiff or floppy? What colour is it? Is it deep and lustrous or washed out and pastel? What does it smell like? Musty and old or new and 'chemically'? What do any books and reports look and smell like? Are they unexpectedly light or heavy? If you tidy up old cups and food wrappings, what do these look, feel and smell like? You might also like to move your desk, computer or phone, or perhaps sit in a different place entirely. The important thing is to change as many of the small things as possible within the fifteen minutes without feeling rushed.

If you are an extremely ordered person who believes that a tidy mind has a tidy workplace, then avoid clearing up for a day. Simply leave everything where you first put it down. What does it feel like? Where in your body are the urges to tidy up located? In your hands, arms or stomach? Is it annoying or disgusting? Do you feel unclean or slovenly? Or do you, perhaps, feel more relaxed, sanguine or energised?

If any of these tasks triggers memories or urges, simply observe them and the pull they exert for a few moments before returning to what you were doing. Only carry out this Habit Releaser for fifteen minutes. The idea is not to create a pristine environment, or to mess it up, but to experience the process of changing your surroundings and to observe how it alters your approach to your day. You can, of course, repeat this exercise over the coming weeks, but try not to do so at the expense of your meditation practice or the other Habit Releasers.

OTHER HABIT RELEASERS

- Newspaper: change it or stop reading one for a week.

- Don't use social media all day.

- Magazine: buy and read a different one.

- Go vegetarian for a day (or even a week).

- Radio: change channels.

- Use a different typeface when you work on a computer.

- Food: try something you have never eaten before (especially if it has seemingly strange or unexpected ingredients).

- Rationalise email: unsubscribe from one list each day.

- Journey: go somewhere new, or somewhere familiar via a different route.

- Observe your posture every hour (do it for a whole day).

- Go to a public meeting: try the town hall or one organised by a pressure group, political party or NGO.

- Sow some seeds, and then watch them grow to fruition.

- Paint or draw in any medium or style.

- Live sport: go and watch a match, especially if you don't like sport or haven't been in years.

- Do some mindful tidying for fifteen minutes each day for a week (take your time and notice how it feels).

- Charity work: choose any local group (it doesn't have to be particularly 'worthy').

- Read a book: choose a genre you would not normally consider.

- Don't watch TV for a day. How does it feel?

- Give up your favourite drink for a day and try a different one.

- Go to the park and watch the sky for at least thirty minutes.

- Sport: try something new, especially if you would not normally consider it or if you never take part in any sport at all. Have you considered something like yoga, t'ai chi or Pilates?

- Go vegan for a day (or even longer).

- Exercise: try something new such as hiking or cycling.

- Play with a child's toys (Lego or Meccano are ideal).

- Spell: use a dictionary to learn ten new words.

- Cinema: go on your own to watch a film.

- Play a children's game (hopscotch anyone?)

- Drive in a less aggressive manner.

- Music: listen to a different genre.

- Clothes: wear something totally different (especially if you would never normally consider it).

- Theatre: go and see a play.

- Go and deliberately talk to a neighbour.

- Make a child laugh.

- Sing in the bath.

- Be nice to someone you do not like.

- Listen to someone you normally find boring: totally indulge them.

- Get up one hour earlier.

- Go to bed one hour earlier.

- Dance for five minutes alone.

- Make a list of possessions you do not need.

- Recycle or give away something (or perhaps several things) you no longer need.

- Turn your mobile off for a day.

- Learn a new skill.

RESOURCES

TRAINING

Breathworks runs excellent courses through accredited trainers, as does the Oxford Mindfulness Centre. The Mindfulness Exchange runs business-orientated courses.

Breathworks: www.breathworks-mindfulness.org.uk

Oxford Mindfulness Centre: www.oxfordmindfulness.org

Mindfulness Exchange: www.mindfulness-exchange.com

WEBSITES

www.franticworld.com The website to accompany this book and its two bestselling companion volumes, *Mindfulness: A Practical Guide to Finding Peace in a Frantic World* and *Mindfulness for Health: A Practical Guide to Relieving Pain, Reducing Stress and Restoring Wellbeing.* It contains resources to complement this volume. There are links to further meditations and books that you might find useful, plus a section listing upcoming talks, events and retreats.

www.mindfulnessteachersuk.org.uk Contains information about the UK network for mindfulness-based teacher training organisations. This association is dedicated to supporting good practice and integrity in the delivery of mindfulness-based courses in the UK. The network is supported by all the main training organisations in the UK who train teachers to deliver mindfulness-based courses.

www.everyday-mindfulness.org Offers comprehensive help and advice for anyone interested in mindfulness.

www.umassmed.edu/cfm the website of the Center for Mindfulness at the University of Massachusetts Medical School. This organisation pioneered bringing mindfulness into healthcare and was founded by Dr Jon Kabat-Zinn. You can also find tapes/CDs of meditation practices recorded by Jon Kabat-Zinn at www.stressreductiontapes.com.

www.wildmind.org This site offers a comprehensive programme of online meditation instruction and support. It also stocks a wide range of CDs of led practices.

www.mindandlife.org The Mind & Life Institute is a non-profit body dedicated to building a scientific understanding of the mind in order to reduce suffering and promote wellbeing. It was set up by respected scientists, philosophers and religious scholars from some of the world's leading universities. Their website is a great source of news and innovative ideas.

www.bemindful.co.uk Mindfulness-related advice and information (and free courses) for anyone suffering from anxiety, stress or depression. Run by the Mental Health Campaign.

RETREATS

There are many retreat centres offering a range of events in many countries. You will find more information on the internet. Here are a couple of examples:

www.goingonretreat.com

www.gaiahouse.co.uk

AUSTRALIAN AND NEW ZEALAND RESOURCES

Breathworks

www.breathworks-mindfulness.net   Contains   details   of Breathworks courses in Sydney.

Meditation centres

www.sydneybuddhistcentre.org.au

www.melbournebuddhistcentre.org.au

www.dharma.org.au

Other online resources of interest

www.openground.com.au For information on mindfulness courses and training around Australia.

www.mindfulexperience.org The home of The Mindfulness Research Guide – a comprehensive resource that provides information to researchers and practitioners on the scientific study of mindfulness, including research publications, measurement tools and mindfulness research centres. It also hosts the *Mindfulness Research Monthly* bulletin for the purpose of keeping researchers and practitioners informed of current advances in research.

FURTHER READING

Burch, V. & Penman, D., *Mindfulness for Health: A Practical Guide to Relieving Pain, Reducing Stress and Restoring Wellbeing* (Piatkus, 2013). Published as *You Are Not Your Pain* in the USA and Canada by Flatiron Books. This includes an eight-week programme to help reduce chronic pain and to help with the suffering and stress associated with long-term illnesses. In 2014 it won the British Medical Association's Best Book (Popular Medicine) Award.

Williams, M. & Penman, D., *Mindfulness: A Practical Guide to Finding Peace in a Frantic World* (Piatkus, 2011). Published by Rodale in the USA and Canada as *Mindfulness: An Eight-Week Plan for Finding Peace in a Frantic World*. This includes an eight-week programme to help you break the cycle of anxiety, stress, depression and mental exhaustion that may be inhibiting your life. Scientific trials show that the programme in the book is highly effective and is on a par with drugs and counselling.

The selection below is meant as an introduction and as an invitation to explore. Many of these teachers and authors have written more books than are listed here and have meditation downloads, apps or CDs you can buy.

CREATIVITY AND DECISION MAKING

Ariely, D., *Predictably Irrational* (HarperCollins, 2009).

Cameron, J., *The Artist's Way* (Pan, 1995).

Duhigg, D., *The Power of Habit* (Random House, 2013).

Kahneman, D., *Thinking Fast and Slow* (Allen Lane, 2011).

Hanson, R., *Buddha's Brain* (New Harbinger, 2009).

Ie, A. et al. (editors) *The Wiley Blackwell Handbook of Mindfulness* (John Wiley & Sons, 2014).

Lamott, A., *Bird by Bird* (Anchor Books, 1995).

Langer, E. J., *On Becoming An Artist* (Ballantine Books, 2006).

Langer, E. J., *Counterclockwise* (Hodder & Stoughton, 2010).

Langer, E. J., *Mindfulness* (A Merloyd Lawrence Book, 1989).

Langer, E. J., *The Power of Mindful Learning* (Da Capo Press Inc., 1998).

McGilchrist, I., *The Master and His Emissary* (Yale University Press, 2009).

MEDITATION, HEALTH AND PSYCHOLOGY

Bennett-Goleman, T., *Emotional Alchemy: How the Mind Can Heal the Heart* (Harmony Books, 2001).

Bertherat, T. & Bernstein, C., *The Body Has its Reasons* (Healing Arts Press, 1989).

Crane, R., *Mindfulness-Based Cognitive Therapy* (Routledge, 2008).

Dahl, J. & Lundgren, T., *Living Beyond Your Pain* (New Harbinger, 2006).

Farhi, D., *The Breathing Book* (Henry Holt & Company, 1996).

Germer, C., *The Mindful Path to Self-Compassion: Freeing Yourself from Destructive Thoughts and Emotions* (Guilford Press, 2009).

Gilbert, P., *The Compassionate Mind: A New Approach to Life'sChallenges* (Constable & Robinson, 2010).

Gilbert, P. & Chodon, *Mindful Compassion* (Robinson, 2013).

Goldstein, J. & Kornfield, J., *Seeking the Heart of Wisdom* (Shambhala Classics, 1987).

Goleman, D., *Emotional Intelligence* (Bantam Books, 1995).

Goleman, D., *Destructive Emotions: How Can We Overcome Them? A Scientific Dialogue with the Dalai Lama* (Bantam Books, 2004).

Goleman, D., *Working with Emotional Intelligence* (Bantam Books, 1998).

Harris, R., *The Happiness Trap* (Constable & Robinson, 2008).

Kabat-Zinn, J., *Coming to Our Senses* (Piatkus, 2005).

Kabat-Zinn, J., *Full Catastrophe Living* (Piatkus, 2001).

Klein, A., *Chronic Pain: The Complete Guide to Relief* (Carroll & Graf, 2001).

Neff, K., *Self-Compassion: Stop Beating Yourself Up and Leave Insecurity Behind* (HarperCollins, 2011).

Santorelli, S., *Heal Thy Self: Lessons on Mindfulness in Medicine* (Three Rivers Press, 2000).

Segal, Z., Williams, M. & Teasdale, J., *Mindfulness-based Cognitive Therapy for Depression: A New Approach for Preventing Relapse* (Guilford Press, 2002).

Smith, S. & Hayes, S., *Get Out of Your Mind and Into Your Life: The New Acceptance and Commitment Therapy* (New Harbinger Publications, 2005).

Williams, M., Segal, Z., Teasdale, J. & Kabat-Zinn, J., *The Mindful Way Through Depression: Freeing Yourself from Chronic Unhappiness* (Guilford Press, 2007).

MEDITATION AND MINDFULNESS

Goldstein, J., *Insight Meditation: The Practice of Freedom* (Newleaf, 1994).

Goldstein, J. & Salzberg, S., *Insight Meditation: A Step-by-step Course on How to Meditate* (Sounds True Inc., 2002).

Hart, W., *Vipassana Meditation: The Art of Living as Taught by S.N Goenka* (HarperCollins, 1987).

Kabat-Zinn, J., *Wherever You Go, There You Are: Mindfulness Meditation in Everyday Life* (Piatkus, 2004).

Kamalashila, *Meditation: Buddhist Way of Tranquillity and Insight* (Windhorse Publications, 2003).

Paramananda, *Change Your Mind* (Windhorse Publications, 1996).

Rosenberg, L., *Breath by Breath* (Thorsons, 1998).

Salzberg, S., *Lovingkindness: The Revolutionary Art of Happiness* (Shambhala Publications, 2004).

Sangharakshita, *Living with Awareness* (Windhorse Publications, 2003).

Wellings, N., *Why Can't I Meditate?* (Piatkus, 2015).

Williams, M. & Kabat-Zinn, J., *Mindfulness: Diverse Perspectives on Its Meaning, Origins and Applications* (Routledge, 2013).

PAIN

Bernhard, T., *How to be Sick* (Wisdom Publications, 2010).

Bond, M. & Simpson, K., *Pain: Its Nature and Treatment* (Elsevier, 2006).

Burch, V., *Living Well with Pain and Illness: Using Mindfulness to Free Yourself from Suffering* (Piatkus, 2008).

Cole, F., Macdonald, H., Carus, C. & Howden-Leach, H., *Overcoming Chronic Pain* (Constable & Robinson, 2005).

Nicholas, M., Molloy, A., Tonkin, L. & Beeston, L., *Manage Your Pain* (Souvenir Press, 2003).

Padfield, D., *Perceptions of Pain* (Dewi Lewis Publications, 2003).

Rosenbaum, E., *Here for Now: Living Well with Cancer through Mindfulness* (Satya House Publications, 2007).

Sadler, J., *Pain Relief without Drugs* (Healing Arts Press, 2007).

Wall, P., *Pain: The Science of Suffering* (Columbia University Press, 2000).

Wall, P. & Melzack, R., *The Challenge of Pain* (Penguin Books, 1982).

INDEX